RETIRE BY 30

RETIRE BY 30

Achieve Financial Freedom Through the
FIRE Movement & Live Life on Your Own Terms

FRANK NIU

PAGE STREET
PUBLISHING CO.

PAGE STREET
PUBLISHING CO.

Copyright © 2024 Frank Niu
First published in 2024 by
Page Street Publishing Co.
27 Congress Street, Suite 1511
Salem, MA 01970
www.pagestreetpublishing.com

Distributed by Macmillan, sales in Canada by The Canadian Manda Group.

28   27   26   25   24   1   2   3   4   5

ISBN-13: 978-1-64567-948-6
ISBN-10: 1-64567-948-9

Library of Congress Control Number: 2023936746

Edited by Marissa Giambelluca
Cover and book design by Emma Hardy for Page Street Publishing Co.

Printed and bound in the United States of America

Dedicated to Annie, who agreed to "in sickness and in health," before realizing the sickness was my addiction to Pokémon cards.

————

DISCLAIMER

This book is strictly intended for educational and informational purposes.

The insights and strategies I share are based on my own experiences. They are designed to inform and inspire; they do not serve as a substitute for professional financial advice.

Making investments comes with inherent risks, including the possibility of losing part or all of your invested funds. Take careful consideration of all factors before making decisions that could influence your financial future.

By choosing to read this book, you recognize that the author and the publisher will not be held accountable for any decisions you make based on the information provided. The journey to financial independence is a personal endeavor, and ultimately, the accountability for choices made on this path rests solely with you. I provide no promises of any sort.

CONTENTS

Chapter 5

HOW TO MAXIMIZE YOUR INCOME   102

Chapter 6

LIVING BELOW YOUR MEANS   162

INTRODUCTION

Have you ever felt the incessant tug of discontentment tethered to your nine-to-five routine? Have you grappled with the draining demands of traditional work schedules that leave little time for personal interests and relationships? You are not alone.

Stepping into the professional world presented a paradox for me. There was something remarkably empowering about having my own income, a sense of independence that was both liberating and rewarding. Yet, simultaneously, I found the traditional corporate grind particularly exhausting. Waking up to the jarring sound of an alarm clock, being thrust into peak hour traffic and then spending the bulk of my day in an office setting that often felt more like a competitive arena than a collaborative workspace, began to weigh heavily on me. As I grappled with my growing discontent toward traditional work, I stumbled upon a concept that seemed to offer a refreshing alternative: Financial Independence, Retire Early, or as it's popularly known, F.I.R.E.

F.I.R.E. is about liberating oneself from the financial shackles that can bind us to unfulfilling jobs. It's a movement that encourages individuals to strive for financial autonomy, allowing them to retire well before the conventional age. For me, it presented an enticing prospect: Imagine a life in which work is a choice, not a necessity, a life in which the allocation of your time is dictated not by a rigid work schedule, but by your passions and personal interests. As captivating as the concept of F.I.R.E. was, it remained a distant dream, not something I seriously considered pursuing, until a momentous event in my life prompted a profound shift in my perspective.

My grandmother's unfortunate passing served as a wake up call. It was a deeply emotional time that brought with it a tide of introspection. The stress, the headaches, the mundane irritations of work, all seemed rather trivial when weighed against the gravity of such a personal loss. The ephemeral nature of life became strikingly clear, and the thought of spending it ensnared in the rat race seemed increasingly untenable. It made me question my priorities and reflect on the true purpose of my existence. Was it to endlessly toil away in an office job? What was the point of it all? This personal tragedy catalyzed a transformative change in my perspective. I resolved to take the reins of my life into my own hands. This set the stage for my journey toward F.I.R.E., propelling me to redefine my relationship with work.

I envisioned a life not controlled by a corporate clock but characterized by flexibility and freedom. I pictured a life of pursuing personal interests that sparked joy, free from financial obligations. The liberty to work on projects that aligned with my values, prioritizing relationships and personal growth over professional demands, became my aspiration. Financial independence underpinned my vision for a life in which choices were made based on what mattered to me, not financial necessity.

Attaining financial independence isn't easy. It requires dedication, calculated planning and, at times, sacrifices. However, with the correct knowledge and a steadfast resolve to implement it, I can assure you that early retirement is within your grasp. In this book, I aim to guide you on the same transformative path, providing you with a roadmap toward retiring early. You'll gain real-life insights and strategies for implementing the three fundamental tenets for achieving F.I.R.E.:

Maximize Your Income: The first tenet involves optimizing your income. This means harnessing your unique skill set, knowledge base and time to amplify your earnings. The logic here is quite straightforward: the more you earn, the more you can allocate toward savings and investments, thereby hastening your course.

Live Below Your Means: The second cornerstone of early retirement revolves around frugality. It's not necessarily about how much you earn, but how much of that income you can successfully retain. This doesn't mean leading an austere lifestyle devoid of joy. Rather, it's about making informed financial decisions, wisely prioritizing your spending and finding happiness in life's simpler pleasures. It involves distinguishing between wants and needs, and recognizing that time is the most precious luxury you possess.

Invest the Difference: The third, and arguably the most pivotal, tenet concerns putting your money to work for you. This is the stage at which the magic of finance comes into play. By judiciously investing the difference between your earnings and expenditures, you unlock the power of compound interest, setting in motion a cycle in which your wealth grows exponentially over time. With a well-structured investment strategy, your money continues to multiply, even when you're asleep, until one day, you accumulate enough wealth to retire from work altogether.

The conventional work structure requires us to trade our time for money, often at the cost of our health and relationships. It's outdated. It's time to rethink, redefine and redesign our relationship with work and money. The clock is ticking, but it's never too late to rewrite your own story. The principles of F.I.R.E. are not just about retiring early; they are about reclaiming your time, your health, your relationships and ultimately, your life.

Join me as we challenge the norm, redefine the role of jobs in our lives and delve into the principles of F.I.R.E. Through my personal journey to retire by 30 and the lessons I've learned, I aim to guide you on your path. The time to act is now. Let's not just dream about financial independence and early retirement; let's strive to make it our reality.

Chapter 1

MY F.I.R.E. JOURNEY

Let's journey back to where it all started. My roots are in the expansive and culturally vibrant nation of China, and it was from there that, at the tender age of four, I migrated to the United States. My family's tale is one of modest beginnings and perseverance. My father's lineage, especially, was entrenched in impoverishment. My grandfather was a peasant, a son of the earth, who, despite his toil, could not read nor write. My father, however, was a man imbued with resolve and grit. He was fueled by an aspiration to shatter the cycle of poverty that had held his lineage in its grip for generations. An ardent scholar, he plunged into his academics with such fervor that he could reel off entire texts from memory. His tireless quest for knowledge and unwavering dedication to his education eventually paid off when he landed a full scholarship to a doctoral program in America shortly after I was born.

In the meantime, I remained anchored in China. While my parents had made significant strides in their personal journey, they were not yet financially positioned to bring me along. For context, graduate students are usually granted a stipend sufficient to cover basic living costs, but not much else. Consequently, I stayed under the care of my grandparents in China until my parents were financially equipped to sustain a child in America. This chapter of my life, though fraught with challenges, played a pivotal role in molding my identity.

As I grew, I fit snugly into the archetype of the overachieving Asian student. In a stroke of genius, my parents crafted a unique strategy to stoke my academic motivation. They would incentivize me with five dollars for every A I achieved, but there was a flip side: every B would trigger a deduction. This system proved to be a potent motivator and worked brilliantly to my advantage. I upheld an almost flawless academic record, receiving only a solitary B throughout my educational journey until my senior year of high school.

My parents' primary focus was on meeting our essential needs. They worked relentlessly to support our family, but when it came to pivotal life decisions, I found myself largely navigating uncharted territory on my own. This came into acute focus when it was time to select a university. I was fortunate to receive acceptances from several institutions, but the decision was anything but straightforward. On one side, I had the chance to attend a local state school, which had extended a full scholarship. This option dangled the promise of a robust education without the specter of student loans looming. Conversely, I could choose a more illustrious institution, a choice that would undoubtedly open new doors but would saddle me with a hefty amount of debt. After ample introspection and careful evaluation of the pros and cons, I decided to enroll in the local state school. The prospect of graduating without a millstone of debt around my neck was appealing, and I was also mindful of sparing my parents any further financial burden.

Much like many 17-year-olds standing on the precipice of adulthood, I found myself grappling with pivotal life decisions: namely, determining my life path and choosing a field of study for college. My interests were eclectic, but one hobby that took up a substantial chunk of my time was playing video games. I was so enraptured by the digital universe of gaming that I ended up with lasting nerve damage in my right hand, a consequence of an era when ergonomics didn't receive the attention it's paid today.

The state institution I chose for my higher studies was renowned for its robust engineering program. Given my obsession with computer games, the field of computer engineering seemed a natural fit. It was an organic confluence of my interests and abilities, and quite unknowingly, I found myself slipping into the tech sphere. It's important to note that during this period, the tech industry didn't carry the sheen of appeal or popularity it commands today. In 2009, the engineering degree associated with the highest earnings was chemical engineering. However, after enduring a semester of Chemistry 101, an experience I found extraordinarily tedious, I knew it wasn't my forte.

Despite my firm decision to join the state school, I often found myself caught in the throes of doubt. The "what ifs" would frequently haunt me. What if a more prestigious school could have offered more professional opportunities? Would my school's reputation act as a stumbling block in my career trajectory? In hindsight, it might have held some sway, but not so much that it radically altered the course of my career.

In my freshman year at college, I was resolute in my aim to shine both academically and in leadership capacities. My efforts paid off as I maintained a flawless 4.0 GPA. Simultaneously, I snagged a couple of leadership roles within the school community. My pursuit of these milestones stemmed from my understanding of their potential to enrich my résumé and enhance my chances of securing a coveted internship, a crucial gateway into the professional world. The fruits of my labor materialized when, in my sophomore year, I landed an internship at a multinational technology and consulting company. This professional foray was an enriching journey that armed me with a treasure trove of knowledge and offered me a sneak peek into the professional realm. Remarkably, I accomplished my assigned project within the first month, which left me with ample leisure time for the rest of my internship. My day-to-day schedule consisted of clocking into work, kickstarting automated processes and then luxuriating in the remainder of the day engaged in recreational activities such as playing disc golf with friends.

However, upon resuming university, I made a decision that

would markedly derail my academic track. I immersed myself in the world of a game called *League of Legends*. The game quickly evolved into a fixation, absorbing eight to ten hours of my daily routine. This indulgence in gaming significantly impacted my academic grades. I found myself flunking numerous courses, several of which were essential prerequisites for graduation. The situation escalated to a dire point when I was on the verge of expulsion from my dorm, even as I held the position of president of the dorm hall. Fortunately, I managed to rectify the situation before it spun out of control. I successfully dropped the courses I was failing before the cut-off date, allowing me to retake them at a later point. This encounter was a sharp admonition, emphasizing the importance of restraint and the perils of gaming addiction. It was a bitter pill to swallow, but it was an indispensable lesson.

In my junior year, I had the good fortune to secure another internship at the same company where I had worked the year before. By then, I had accumulated a robust academic record, and I felt assured that my GPA was strong enough to land me a job post-graduation. Consequently, I permitted myself some flexibility to unwind and immerse myself in the college experience. My aim was to sustain a GPA above 3.0, but I dedicated most of my time to indulging in my hobbies, particularly anime and video games. It was during this period that I began to understand the power of good habits. By setting aside regular study hours, seeking help when I was struggling and continuously evaluating my progress,

I ensured my grades remained strong. These habits of discipline, reflection and perseverance became invaluable, and as we delve deeper into the financial aspects later in the book, you'll see how these principles became foundational in my approach to finances.

Upon graduating, I had several job offers at my disposal. These offers encompassed an array of roles, from tech sales positions and consulting roles to opportunities in various software companies. Among these, the offer to join the company where I had interned as a cloud engineer stood out as particularly appealing. The opportunity to work on leading-edge cloud technologies at a tech behemoth was a prospect I couldn't pass up. After a period of negotiation, they extended their final offer: a base salary of $74,000 per year. I also managed to negotiate a signing bonus of $4,000 and they graciously offered to bear my relocation expenses to Boston, which was a significant financial relief.

The job was not particularly demanding—a crisp contrast to the rigorous curriculum I had grown used to during my university years. My typical day would commence around nine in the morning and I'd work on various tasks for a few hours before enjoying a leisurely lunch break. The afternoons were relatively easy and I often wrapped up work early. The job did, however, serve as an excellent springboard for my career. It offered a stable work atmosphere, a supportive team and a platform to refine my skills as a software engineer. I was performing well, consistently receiving positive appraisals from my manager and managing to squirrel away a sizable portion of my earnings. Life was comfortable, predictable and secure.

As time trickled by, I began to harbor a desire for more. I craved novel challenges, a spirited work environment and the chance to test my limits. This yearning for change was further stoked when my girlfriend received a job proposition from Facebook, located in San Francisco. The city, recognized as the technological heart of the world, was brimming with enticing job prospects and a dynamic tech culture. I had always nurtured a dream to work in this bustling metropolis and the possibility of turning this aspiration into reality was alluring. However, I also stood on the verge of a promotion and a substantial pay increase. Choosing between staying or taking on a new adventure presented a significant fork in the road of my professional voyage.

As I grappled with the idea of departing my job, I sought counsel from my parents. Predictably, they expressed their disapproval of this decision. They implored me to follow the path of caution: to persist at my job, maintain a low profile and steadily amass wealth. Their viewpoint stemmed from their desire for stability and security, principles they had adopted since childhood. However, my goal was quite different: To accumulate wealth at an accelerated pace to exercise my own agency in selecting the pursuits that mattered to me. I've always found it grating to be told what to do, and though I didn't know it at the time, F.I.R.E. was what I was working toward.

As the time for performance evaluations loomed, I was imbued with a sense of expectation. I anticipated a promotion and a substantial pay hike as a testament to my dedication and diligence. However, when the evaluation eventually took place, it was a disappointment. There was no promotion, and the pay raise was a meager 1.1%. The promise of a future promotion and pay increase was dangled before me, on the condition that I wait a few more months or even half a year. At this point, my patience was dwindling. I was mentally equipped to explore other opportunities. Interestingly, when I began receiving job propositions from other organizations and informed my manager about my plans to resign, he promptly offered me a notable pay raise in a bid to retain me. This episode was enlightening. It brought to light that my worth to the organization far exceeded what they were paying me. It also highlighted that your earnings don't always mirror your level of contribution to the organization. I observed that some senior members of my team, despite lesser contributions, were earning significantly more than I.

Before I fully immersed myself in my job hunt, I decided to dabble in day trading. The movie *The Wolf of Wall Street* had recently premiered, making trading appear a profitable and simple venture. I thought, "How challenging could it be to trade full time?" Predictably, my excursion into day trading didn't unfold as I had envisioned.

Initially, I enjoyed a run of fortune with penny stocks, managing to double my investment from $2,000 to $4,000. However, as my profits expanded, so did my avarice. I started investing substantial amounts: $15,000, then escalating to $30,000. Predictably, this reckless approach resulted in significant losses, and I found myself receiving a margin call from Fidelity®.

Interestingly, Fidelity undertook a study on their most lucrative traders and the results were quite insightful: The traders with the highest profits were those who had forgotten about their accounts. This underlined the potential risks of day trading and the virtues of long-term investing. It is a well-established fact that 99% of day traders wind up losing money. You may consider yourself part of the privileged 1%, but the reality is the odds are heavily against you. We, as humans, are fundamentally emotional creatures and these emotions frequently spur us to make investment decisions at less-than-ideal moments. I learned this lesson through first-hand experience, albeit the hard way.

After my stint at a large corporation with a heavy focus on processes and protocols, I craved a shift. I yearned for a contrasting environment, one that was more vibrant and less bound by red tape. With this aspiration, I sought opportunities at the smallest startup I could locate. My search guided me to a small fintech company based in Iowa but with a branch in San Francisco. They extended me a job proposition.

However, there was a caveat. The proposal was an "exploding offer," implying that I had a limited window to accept. At the time, I was oblivious to the fact that this was a negotiation strategy frequently employed by companies. I earnestly believed that they would rescind the offer if I sought an extension. Consequently, I forfeited a considerable amount of money by not securing other offers and leveraging them. They offered me a package with a base salary of $130,000, accompanied by a quantity of stock options. Regrettably, the stock options would turn out to be worthless and my girlfriend and I separated before I even moved.

Relocating to San Francisco served as a significant accelerator for my career. Joining a technologically advanced startup exposed me to various contemporary programming concepts, such as test-driven development, microservices and Amazon Web Services. The limited team size implied that I was entrusted with a great deal of responsibility. It was a welcome departure, characterized by its modern tech stack and fast-paced milieu. However, there was a significant obstacle: the company wasn't profitable. The founder attempted to secure funds but was unsuccessful. My tenure lasted less than six months before the company was compelled to implement layoffs. They provided a few weeks of severance, and I found myself jobless for roughly a month.

Unexpectedly, that one month of unemployment turned out to be quite enjoyable. I indulged in numerous dates, participated in meetups and relished life in San Francisco. I wasn't concerned about finances as I had managed to save sufficiently to cover my rent. The job market in San Francisco was thriving. Within a week, I had an array of interviews scheduled and eventually received multiple offers from diverse tech companies. After careful evaluation, I decided to join a mid-stage personal finance startup. It seemed to possess everything that the previous lacked: it was more mature, had substantial funding and was ranked among Glassdoor's top 25 small and medium businesses to work for. The startup atmosphere still appealed to me and it appeared to be the perfect fit. They offered me a base salary of $155,000, coupled with $100,000 in restricted stock units (RSUs). Later, they were acquired, which significantly increased the value of the stocks. I was entrusted with considerably more responsibility, which enabled me to achieve an abundance of work. Despite my achievements on the job front, I found myself increasingly ensnared by the undercurrents of corporate politics. Stress manifested physically, giving me my first migraine ever. Work had consumed such a large chunk of my cognitive bandwidth that it was hard to think of anything else. I discovered F.I.R.E. in an online forum during this period, although it would take the sobering loss of my grandmother to make me consider it earnestly.

The year 2017 marked a watershed moment in the world of cryptocurrencies. Bitcoin, priced at $1,000 at the start of the year, surged to $20,000 by the end. Ethereum, originally worth $50, eclipsed $1,000. Litecoin, initially valued at $4, peaked at more than $400. The crypto market was in an upswing and I was youthful and zealous to seize the moment. I couldn't let this wave pass me by.

Consequently, I decided to step away from my role at the personal finance startup. I embarked on a project independently and after several months, I managed to persuade a few friends to collaborate. Our startup's value proposition revolved around tokenizing equity. I was fervent about the idea and managed to convince my friends that this was the future. I envisioned us becoming exceedingly affluent and revolutionizing the world. However, cryptocurrencies were not widely accepted and we encountered numerous obstacles. We struggled to find lawyers willing to collaborate with us and our engineering backgrounds led us to presume that if we developed an excellent product, users would naturally gravitate toward us. But the reality was far removed from our initial expectations. After months of tireless endeavor, our startup failed to achieve any substantial traction.

A particularly memorable incident during this phase was a call with John McAfee, the infamous British–American entrepreneur and cybersecurity expert. He decided against investing. Our startup's failure was a harsh setback, but the most agonizing aspect of the experience was the unraveling of my friendships with my co-founders. The pressure and disappointment accompanying our venture's collapse strained our relationships and over time, we slowly drifted apart.

During this trying phase, I was in a committed relationship and we were contemplating the idea of purchasing a house. However, the exorbitant real estate prices in San Francisco were well beyond our financial means, leading us to explore other locales. Our search brought us to Chicago, a city with a comparatively affordable housing market. Simultaneously, I received a job offer from a prominent online and mobile food-ordering and delivery marketplace. The total compensation package was approximately $200,000, making the prospect of relocating to Chicago even more enticing. For those unfamiliar with the structure of such offers, they generally consist of a bulk sum of RSUs that vest over four years, with a one-year cliff. Unless you stay with the company for a minimum of a year, you don't receive any portion of your stock package. As fortune would have it, the stock hit record highs right when I reached my one-year vesting period, resulting in my total compensation for the year amounting to approximately $300,000.

Residing in Chicago proved to be considerably economical, particularly compared to the inflated living costs in San Francisco. We rented a rather spacious one-bedroom apartment at roughly $1,900 per month, a bargain compared to the prices we were accustomed to. The city had myriad offerings, notably a diverse food scene, and the summers were utterly charming. We exchanged rings and vows in 2018, starting our married life. With the funds accrued from selling my stock, we started to seriously mull the prospect of purchasing a house in the Windy City. However, that year we also witnessed the advent of the polar vortex, a climatic event causing extraordinarily cold temperatures. The weather conditions were so brutal that advisories against stepping outdoors due to potential lung damage were issued. This episode led us to rethink our decision to plant roots in Chicago, as we debated whether we were equipped to weather such severe winters.

We started contemplating a return to California, primarily fueled by the yearning for a milder climate, but also due to the abundance of job opportunities in the Golden State. We felt assured that even if my forthcoming role didn't pan out, securing a new job in California wouldn't pose a substantial hurdle given the state's thriving tech industry.

Armed with the experience from prior job interviews and negotiations, I found the job-hunting process significantly smoother this time. I received preliminary offers from budding tech companies in Los Angeles. However, the offers were relatively modest, falling within the $200,000 range, which was less than my compensation at the time. This was somewhat disappointing, as I had anticipated a significant increase in my earnings. I then received an offer from an e-commerce company in New York, at approximately $250,000. I was also interviewing with several other tech companies. Until then, I hadn't seriously contemplated securing a position at a FAANG (Facebook, Amazon, Apple, Netflix, Google) company. However, witnessing my friends landing roles at these high-profile companies on LinkedIn prompted me to recognize that I was equally capable. All I needed was to exert more effort or enhance my study to clinch these roles.

The FAANG interviews were the most rigorous I had undergone, stretching over two days. The first day was primarily technical, encompassing system design questions and other specialized queries. The second day focused predominantly on behavioral aspects, with an emphasis on culture-fit questions to ensure I comprehended the environment I would be stepping into. The offer I received was markedly higher than the others. The total compensation package was more than $500,000, a figure that seemed astounding to me at the time. One of the other facets that lured me, apart from the substantial compensation package, was the company's work culture, with a goal of prioritizing people over process. The company esteemed agility and swiftness, and a prevalent adage within the organization was "freedom and responsibility." You're granted the liberty to make your own decisions, but you're also expected to take responsibility should things not proceed as anticipated.

We migrated back to the Bay Area for my role, which was genuinely a wonderful work environment. It was essentially the job of my dreams. I had finally landed a role at a FAANG company and was receiving a considerable salary. During this period, my wife and I succeeded in saving more than half of our earnings, which we invested. We also initiated our search to purchase our first home in San Jose. Then, the COVID-19 pandemic struck.

Cities worldwide enforced lockdown measures in a bid to limit the virus's spread, and the stock market witnessed a significant dip. The fluctuation in the markets and subsequent recovery was a period of massive wealth redistribution, likely one of the most substantial in our lifetimes, and we were fortunate enough to be in a position to continue investing during this time. As we steered this financial course, we witnessed nearly every asset class, including real estate, cryptocurrencies, stocks and even collectible card games, attain near all-time highs.

We had originally planned to enroll our child in daycare, but with the escalating health crisis, we no longer felt it was a safe option. We informed our nanny of our decision to assume full-time care of our child ourselves and switched to a remote working arrangement. At the pandemic's onset, we, like many, assumed that this situation might only last a few months and that life would revert to normal by the summer. Our lease was due to expire around this time and we contemplated a temporary move to Canada to leverage childcare support from family members residing there, with plans to return once the pandemic had eased.

The situation's uncertainty was intimidating and we found ourselves continuously reevaluating our plans and making modifications to accommodate the swiftly changing circumstances. The pandemic had upended our lives, but we were committed to navigating these testing times, placing the safety and well-being of our family at the forefront.

Not long after we had started adapting to the new normal ushered in by the pandemic, we suffered a heartrending loss. My wife's twin sister, a cherished family member, tragically passed away. The news was a shock, sending ripples of grief through our family. We were left struggling with an overwhelming sense of loss and sorrow, a pain especially acute for my wife, who had shared an exceptional bond with her twin sister. Besides the emotional upheaval, we were suddenly plunged into the intricate and often overwhelming logistics accompanying the demise of a loved one. Funeral arrangements had to be made, legal matters addressed and personal belongings sorted. Each task was a stinging reminder of the void left by her departure. The process was strenuous, filled with moments of melancholy and introspection. We found ourselves sailing through a sea of grief while simultaneously handling the practical aspects of our loss. It was a challenging period, one that tested our resilience and fortitude as a family. However, throughout it all, we held onto each other, deriving comfort and strength from our shared grief and recollections of happier times.

In the midst of this trying time, we also welcomed the birth of our second son. My paternity leave was an extraordinary experience. I had the special privilege of witnessing all the firsts of my child's life. Despite the unavoidable fatigue and challenges that come with caring for an infant, the joy and satisfaction it brought were unmatched. I had always envisioned $2,000,000 as the magical sum that would afford me a comfortable retirement. During my paternity leave, our net worth, excluding the value of our primary residence, exploded past this threshold. According to the 4%

rule (page 44), we could spend approximately $80,000 annually without draining our savings, thus achieving early retirement. These invaluable family moments, coupled with our financial prosperity, made me realize that the quest for financial independence and early retirement could be nearing its conclusion.

During my scheduled paternity leave, I received an unanticipated call from my manager. To provide some background, it's crucial to mention that there had been considerable shifts in the management hierarchy during my tenure. The entire chain of command, from the vice president to my direct manager, had either chosen to leave or been let go. This instability had persisted during my paternity leave, with both my director and immediate manager leaving the company.

My newly assigned manager got in touch with an air of urgency. She informed me that the team was grappling with significant issues and desperately needed me back at work as soon as possible. However, this request placed me in a challenging situation. At home, I had two young children who were still not vaccinated. In the face of the ongoing pandemic and the tragic loss our family had experienced the previous year, we were unwavering in our commitment to our children's health and safety. I expressed to my manager that the only scenario in which I could consider an early return was if an infant vaccine was available. Her reaction to my concerns was anything but understanding. She retorted with a harsh ultimatum, threatening to dismiss me without severance if I didn't return to work within a week. Astonishingly, she even conspired with the Human Resources (HR) department to retroactively change my paternity leave dates. I only discovered this deceitful maneuver when I received an automated email from our HR software system.

Seeking an explanation, I contacted our employee services team, who confirmed that it was indeed my HR business partner who had instigated the change. This predicament served as a distinct reminder of the brutal truths of corporate politics and the lengths some individuals would go to place business needs above their employees' personal circumstances and well-being.

In a bid to defuse the situation, my manager emailed me, purporting to be unaware of my paternity leave schedule. This was a puzzling claim, given the abundant evidence. There were exchanged emails, conversations during team meetings and my calendar auto-responses. My Slack status indicated my leave and I had even discussed my plans in one-on-one meetings with my colleagues. All these factors unequivocally validated my original leave dates. The individuals I was negotiating with left me in a profound state of disbelief. It felt like I had been plunged into a graphic novel, battling with antagonists attempting to rewrite history to favor their timeline. They were essentially forcing me to return to work, ignoring my necessity to prioritize my family during the most devastating pandemic of our era.

The matter escalated to the extent that I had to hire an attorney. I felt obliged to lodge a complaint against my manager and the HR business partner to the Employee Relations department. This was a recently formed department in the company, specifically created to deal with such issues. The ensuing month was a tempest of stress and unpredictability as I maneuvered the murky waters of corporate conflict. In the end, the company presented me with two choices: either return to work prematurely or accept a severance package and sever ties entirely. After thoughtful deliberation, I opted for the latter. When confronted with a choice between my profession and my family's health and safety, my family took precedence.

We were indeed fortunate, even blessed, to be financially secure enough to make such a decision. My journey in the technology sector had been relatively successful, filled with accomplishments and milestones to which many aspire. But it was always just a job for me, a means to an end. I didn't have an insatiable passion for computer science, nor did I feel it a compelling vocation. It was a discipline I excelled in, one that offered good prospects, but it was not my ultimate passion.

Throughout our professional lives, my wife and I had always been financially conscientious and disciplined. We regularly saved more than half of our income, living significantly below our means. We invested prudently and patiently, understanding that wealth is built not through rapid money-making schemes, but through steady, long-term investments. This strategy proved successful. At the end of 2021, we finally achieved our financial independence, retire early (F.I.R.E.) goal. It was a moment of victory, a reflection of years of hard work, discipline and sensible financial management.

I now find myself in a state of satisfaction and joy that I have never felt before. I have the luxury of time, the most valuable asset of all. I can be there for my children's milestones, their laughter, their tears and their everyday moments. I can immerse myself in the realm of books. I can indulge my love for anime and media. I have the freedom to do whatever I want, whenever I want. This newfound liberty is immensely freeing. I no longer need to stick to the rigid structure of corporate life, navigate office politics or sacrifice my time and tranquility for a job. I can choose how I spend each day, each hour. This freedom, the ability to live life on my terms, has given me a level of happiness and fulfillment I have never known before. It's a life I wouldn't exchange for anything else.

Chapter 2

WHAT IS F.I.R.E.?

F.I.R.E. Definition

The F.I.R.E. movement has emerged as a transformative approach to personal finance, challenging traditional views of work, retirement and financial planning. More than just an economic strategy, F.I.R.E. reimagines how we relate to money and shapes our life choices in alignment with personal values and aspirations. We'll discuss the core principles of F.I.R.E., from financial independence and early retirement to its accessibility and flexibility across various demographics. We will also delve into the practicalities of planning for retirement, particularly focusing on the 4% rule: a foundational concept that guides retirement spending.

Financial independence, at the core of F.I.R.E., is not merely living without a regular paycheck. It's an all-encompassing philosophy that transcends mere financial security, enabling one to achieve a stage at which income from assets such as savings and investments comfortably covers all expenses. But this independence means more than meeting daily needs or financial emergencies;

it embodies liberation from financial constraints. This autonomy paves the way for a life in which career decisions are not dictated by salary alone. The freedom to spend time with family, travel, pursue hobbies or even explore new career paths is no longer restricted by traditional financial obligations. What would you do if money were no object? How could financial independence align your life with your personal values, desires and aspirations?

Take Tom and Emily, a middle-class couple in their mid-30s, who were living a typical suburban life. They had good jobs, a comfortable home and a stable routine, yet they both felt a yearning for something more. The idea of waiting until their 60s to retire and finally explore the world seemed almost unbearable. Introduced to F.I.R.E. principles by a friend, they began to live frugally and invest wisely. After fifteen years of perseverance, Tom and Emily retired in their early 50s. They sold their house, packed their bags and embarked on their dream journey. Their travels were not a perpetual vacation but a way of life that fulfilled them in ways they had never anticipated. They blogged about their experiences, inspiring others to consider what financial independence could mean for them.

With F.I.R.E., early retirement takes this independence to a new level, offering an exit from the conventional work scene much earlier than the standard retirement age. It's not merely about leaving work; it's an empowering choice to embrace a lifestyle that emphasizes balance, growth, joy and fulfillment. Whether that means exploring new places, engaging in hobbies, focusing on family or venturing into personally rewarding vocations, early retirement reflects a life in which work complements, not overshadows, other pursuits.

Consider Greg, a highly talented engineer. Fresh out of college, he quickly made a name for himself in the tech industry. His innovative thinking and relentless work ethic led him to the forefront of several breakthrough projects. Yet, beneath the professional success lays a growing fear of burnout. The late nights and endless cycles of high-pressure projects began to weigh on Greg. He loved his job but found himself increasingly stressed, with little time for family or personal pursuits. The F.I.R.E. movement offered him a plan for an early and flexible retirement. By his early 40s, Greg retired. He was free to choose his projects and working hours, focusing on innovation and creativity rather than deadlines and bottom lines. His family life blossomed as well. Greg now spends quality time with his spouse and children, building deeper connections and creating cherished memories.

Think F.I.R.E. is only for the wealthy? Think again. Many people initially believe that the F.I.R.E. movement is only attainable for those with six-figure salaries or a substantial inheritance. They think that it requires an extravagant lifestyle cutback or access to high-level investment opportunities. This common misconception can deter individuals from even considering the approach, thinking it is out of reach for them. F.I.R.E.'s accessibility transcends income levels, opening doors for people from all walks of life. You don't have to follow every aspect of F.I.R.E. to meet your financial goals. For instance, you may decide to prioritize financial freedom instead of early retirement. Embracing F.I.R.E. doesn't necessarily mean early retirement for everyone. For some, especially those in lower income brackets, financial independence might translate into greater financial security, flexibility in work choices or the freedom to pursue passions without immediate economic pressures.

Maya, a single mother in her early 30s, was doing her best to balance work, parenting and finances. Living in an urban environment with a modest salary, she often found herself stretched thin, working long hours and still struggling to make ends meet. Though she wasn't earning a six-figure salary, she found inspiration in the F.I.R.E. movement's inclusive approach. By living frugally and learning about wise investing practices, Maya created a more robust financial foundation for herself and her daughter, Lily. Years passed, and Maya's disciplined approach began to pay off. Her investments grew and she built an emergency fund that provided a safety net. While early retirement was not her goal, the financial independence she achieved gave her flexibility and peace of mind. She was able to work fewer hours, spend more quality time with Lily and even pursue a part-time degree to improve her career prospects.

The transformative power of the F.I.R.E. movement lies in its adaptability. From traveling the world to balancing work and life, to finding financial stability in challenging circumstances, F.I.R.E. offers a guiding light. It invites us to engage with money in a way that reflects our unique goals, circumstances and values. Whether the aspiration is to retire decades ahead of schedule or simply to build a more robust financial foundation, the principles of F.I.R.E. resonate universally. It's a movement not just about economics but about living life on our own terms.

Flavors of F.I.R.E.

Various subcategories and approaches have evolved to cater to different lifestyles, income levels and financial goals. Three common subcategories of F.I.R.E. are LeanF.I.R.E., BaristaF.I.R.E. and FatF.I.R.E.

LeanF.I.R.E. attracts those who see beauty in simplicity and who are willing to adopt a minimalist approach to financial independence and early retirement. LeanF.I.R.E. is a lifestyle choice, a philosophy that prioritizes living with less to achieve freedom sooner. This approach requires cutting expenses to the bare minimum, carefully budgeting and often choosing to reside in areas with a lower cost of living. While LeanF.I.R.E. offers the allure of financial independence without needing a large nest egg, it is not without challenges. The absence of a substantial financial cushion might make unforeseen expenses a serious concern. Moreover, continuous frugality might lead to feelings of deprivation for some, and significant lifestyle adjustments might be needed that aren't suited to everyone. Therefore, those considering LeanF.I.R.E. must weigh the joy of earlier freedom against potential financial and lifestyle constraints in the present.

BaristaF.I.R.E. represents a middle path that seeks to blend the desire for early retirement with a more balanced and gradual approach. This strategy often involves leaving a stressful, full-time job but continuing with part-time work or pursuing a passion project that might not pay as well. The name "BaristaF.I.R.E." points to the idea that one could work a lower paying but more flexible job, like being a barista, which still provides essential benefits such as health insurance. While this approach offers a smoother transition into full retirement, it might present its challenges. Income uncertainty might arise and there is a risk of becoming overly dependent on part-time roles for necessary benefits. This method might appeal most to those who desire a slower pace without completely cutting ties to the professional world.

FatF.I.R.E., on the other end of the spectrum, is geared toward individuals who have grown accustomed to a certain standard of living and wish to maintain or even enhance it during retirement. This strategy requires diligent financial planning, higher earnings and often more aggressive investment strategies. It enables lifestyle continuation with a more significant buffer for unexpected expenses or market fluctuations. However, it's not without potential pitfalls. The drive to achieve FatF.I.R.E. could lead to an overemphasis on material wealth, possibly overshadowing other fulfilling aspects of retirement. Moreover, the need to amass a larger nest egg might delay retirement compared to the other two strategies.

These three categories offer varied paths to financial independence and early retirement. LeanF.I.R.E. appeals to the minimalist, seeking freedom through frugality, whereas FatF.I.R.E. caters to those looking to retire in luxury without sacrificing their current lifestyle. BaristaF.I.R.E. bridges the gap, providing a path for those seeking balance and a more gradual transition. A careful comparison of these approaches reveals subtle nuances and trade-offs. LeanF.I.R.E. might allow for the earliest retirement but may require sacrifices that could affect quality of life. BaristaF.I.R.E. offers a compromise but introduces its own complexities, such as reliance on part-time work. FatF.I.R.E. provides comfort and security but might necessitate longer working years and a relentless focus on financial growth.

Your choice among LeanF.I.R.E., BaristaF.I.R.E. and FatF.I.R.E. is deeply personal. While there are distinct characteristics for each, it's essential to recognize that they exist on a spectrum, and it's not a strict binary choice. Your selection will be influenced by your individual preferences, risk tolerance, values and financial situation. By understanding the unique characteristics and potential challenges of each, you can choose a path that resonates with your aspirations and lifestyle.

How Much Money Do You Need? The 4% Rule

Having explored the diverse applications and philosophical underpinnings of the F.I.R.E. movement, it's crucial to delve into the practical mechanics that make it all possible. One of the most important concepts that enable financial independence and early retirement is a carefully planned approach to spending during retirement. This leads us to an essential component of the F.I.R.E. strategy, known as the 4% rule. A well-calibrated guideline for sustainable withdrawal rates, the 4% rule provides the mathematical backbone that supports the dreams and aspirations outlined in the F.I.R.E. movement. Let's take a closer look at how this rule operates and how it can be tailored to various financial scenarios.

Suppose you aspire to spend $100,000 every year during retirement. In accordance with the 4% rule, you'd need an investment portfolio worth $2,500,000 to sustain such spending indefinitely. If we presume that your investment portfolio would grow at an annual rate of 7% and you withdraw only 4% per year, then theoretically your assets will continue to increase over time, never depleting. For a more cautious approach, you could withdraw less, perhaps 3%. Historically, the S&P 500 has generated an average annual return of 10%, assuming reinvestment of dividends.

From the second year of retirement onward, you adjust your withdrawal amount in line with inflation. Why is inflation important? Because it gradually reduces your purchasing power. As the cost of living rises, if you continue to spend the same amount, your standard of living will effectively decrease. Therefore, it's essential to adjust your withdrawal amount according to inflation. For instance, if inflation is at 2%, you would withdraw $100,000 x 1.02, which equals $102,000 for that year's expenses.

Conversely, during periods of deflation, you would withdraw less. For example, 2% deflation would result in a withdrawal of $100,000 x 0.98 = $98,000. This process is cumulative; each year's withdrawal is adjusted based on the previous year's figure and the current inflation rate.

But, is this strategy foolproof? What about periods of economic downturns and stock market slumps? The 4% rule, also referred to as the "Bengen rule," was proposed by retired financial advisor William P. Bengen. Assuming a portfolio allocation of 50% stocks (the S&P 500) and 50% bonds (intermediate term Treasuries), Bengen tested his theory using historical data from 1926 through 1992.

Here's a summary of his results:

- With a 3% withdrawal rate, all portfolios lasted 50 years post-retirement.
- With a 4% withdrawal rate, most portfolios lasted 50 years. Even for those who retired during the ten most challenging years, the portfolios lasted at least 35 years.
- With a 5% withdrawal rate, more than half of the portfolios didn't last 50 years, but even the worst-performing ones still lasted at least 20 years.
- With a 6% withdrawal rate, only 7 portfolios lasted 50 years and 10 portfolios lasted less than 20 years.

- Bengen's study also found that the 50/50 allocation was only ideal if the sole objective was to maximize portfolio longevity. If retirees wanted to enhance their wealth during retirement, a greater percentage of allocation toward stocks was suggested, potentially up to 75%.

The concept of a safe withdrawal rate has been widely integrated into the operations of the financial services industry, being accepted and utilized by numerous major financial firms. A convenient method to estimate your required retirement target is by multiplying your anticipated yearly expenses by 25. This equation provides the same results, yet it is a bit more straightforward to comprehend. For instance, if your estimated annual expenditure is $100,000, multiply that by 25 and you get $2.5 million.

As we all know, the future is filled with uncertainties and it's impossible to make assurances about investment returns. However, the 4% rule has proven its resilience over time, demonstrating its effectiveness even if you had begun your retirement immediately before significant financial crises such as the Great Depression, World War II or the period of stagnation and inflation in the 1970s. By trimming your withdrawal rate to 3%, you further enhance your financial security during retirement.

There are alternative strategies, such as implementing a dynamic withdrawal rate, which can further boost your chances of sustaining your retirement savings. If you manage to reduce your yearly withdrawal rate by a mere 5% during periods of financial downturns, it significantly improves your ability to weather market turbulence. In a bear market, the market is faced with extended periods of falling prices. This term generally describes situations where securities tumble by 20% or more from their recent peaks, driven largely by pervasive negativity and souring investor moods. So, using the same initial figures, during the most challenging years of a bear market, you'd withdraw $95,000 as opposed to $100,000. This not only helps conserve your retirement fund but also provides you with an extra buffer for the future, possibly enabling you to increase your withdrawal amount when the market recovers.

The F.I.R.E. movement is far more than a financial trend; it is a lifestyle choice that resonates with a diverse array of individuals seeking autonomy, fulfillment and balance in their lives. Through its emphasis on financial independence and the empowering option of early retirement, F.I.R.E. encourages a thoughtful alignment of personal values with financial goals. By debunking common misconceptions, understanding the practicalities of the 4% rule and recognizing the movement's adaptability, we can see that F.I.R.E. offers a universally appealing pathway toward a secure and fulfilling financial future. Whether you're looking to retire decades ahead of schedule or seeking greater control and flexibility, the lessons of the F.I.R.E. movement provide valuable insights that extend beyond mere economics into the very fabric of our lives.

Chapter 3

PITFALLS TO AVOID

Attaining financial independence requires a delicate balance, necessitating not only the implementation of sound financial strategies, but also the evasion of harmful financial practices. The road to early retirement is not simply about making the right decisions, such as disciplined saving, prudent investing and living frugally. It also involves actively avoiding harmful ones, like frivolous expenditure, risky investment ventures and accumulating excessive debt. This dual method is vital in accruing and preserving wealth over an extended period.

Get-Rich-Quick Schemes

Charles Ponzi, an Italian immigrant to the United States, masterminded one of the most notorious fraudulent investment operations in the 1920s, eventually giving rise to the name "Ponzi scheme." Ponzi's operation was hinged on a promise that was irresistible: a 50% return on investment within 45 days or double the investment in 90 days. The mechanism behind this extraordinary return was seemingly based on arbitrage opportunities in international reply coupons used for overseas postage. However, beneath this facade of legitimacy lay a fraud of epic proportions. Ponzi wasn't capitalizing on arbitrage opportunities as he had claimed. He relied on a continuous influx of new investors and used their contributions to pay off earlier investors, creating an illusion of legitimacy and profitability. As the scheme gained momentum, so did Ponzi's wealth and stature. He lived a life of luxury, basking in the spotlight and projecting an image of success and affluence.

However, this remarkable growth was a house of cards waiting to collapse. Ponzi's operation was fundamentally unsustainable. The promise of high returns required an ever-growing pool of new investors. As the scheme expanded, it became increasingly challenging to attract enough new capital to maintain the illusion of profitability. The tipping point came when the *Boston Post* began investigating Ponzi's operations, leading to a panic among investors who tried to cash out their investments. The fallout from the collapse of Ponzi's scheme was catastrophic. Thousands of investors who had given Ponzi their life savings were left in financial ruin. The total losses from Ponzi's scheme were estimated to be approximately $20 million, equivalent to $250 million today. Ponzi himself ended up in prison and died in poverty.

While traditional Ponzi schemes are less prevalent today, investors need to be vigilant and adept at identifying and sidestepping today's nuanced financial scams. In more recent times, several multi-level marketing (MLM) companies have been accused of operating as disguised pyramid schemes. These companies often sell legitimate products but make most of their profits from recruitment rather than sales. Participants are encouraged to recruit others into the scheme, with the promise of earning a commission from their recruits' sales. However, such systems are destined to fail as the recruitment pool inevitably dries up, leaving those at the bottom of the pyramid with significant losses. Some high-profile MLM companies have faced lawsuits and regulatory actions due to these deceptive practices.

Despite the changing times and evolving tactics, the fundamental structure of these get-rich-quick schemes remains the same: They promise fast and easy money but lead to financial ruin. We live in an era in which the promise of instant riches is marketed to us from every direction. From lottery tickets to online advertisements, the allure of acquiring wealth quickly and effortlessly is a seductive trap many fall into. I'm here to dispel the myth of "easy money" and provide a reality check on get-rich-quick schemes. Despite their enticing nature, get-rich-quick schemes are fundamentally flawed in their promise of delivering fast wealth with minimal effort. They prey on our human weaknesses—greed, fear and the yearning for immediate gratification.

Understanding the anatomy of a get-rich-quick scheme is an integral part of equipping oneself against falling prey to their allure. At their core, these schemes are intricate webs of deception, meticulously crafted to mimic the facade of legitimate business opportunities or promising investment strategies. The schemes' architects excel at masking their nefarious intentions with a veil of respectability. They artfully use the jargon and structure of valid enterprises, offering potential "partnerships" or "memberships" in what appears to be a lucrative business or a promising startup. It's not uncommon for them to produce polished promotional materials, such as glossy brochures, professional websites and compelling testimonials, which create an illusion of legitimacy. Once they've grabbed your attention, the schemers employ aggressive, high-pressure sales techniques designed to push you into making a hasty decision. These tactics might involve limited-time offers, exclusive "seats" or "slots" or purported insider information. By creating a false sense of scarcity or urgency, they aim to pressure you into acting quickly, without giving you the time for proper due diligence or consultation. Another common characteristic of these schemes is their use of ambiguous language and dense, unreadable fine print. The actual "deal" or "offer" is often buried under convoluted legal vernacular and complex terms and conditions that are hard to decipher. This tactic serves to obscure the fact that the proposed business model or investment strategy is fundamentally flawed, unsustainable or downright illegal.

To understand the bleak reality of these schemes, let's look at some revealing statistics and data. A report by the Federal Trade Commission (FTC) on MLM, a popular format for get-rich-quick schemes, found that a staggering 99% of MLM participants lose money. Yes, you read that right. Ninety-nine out of 100 people who enter such schemes end up losing money rather than making it. Why such dismal numbers? The answer lies in the pyramid-like structure that these schemes often adopt. They are designed in a way that only those few at the very top of the pyramid stand a chance of making significant money, primarily from the influx of new participants joining the scheme. The vast majority of participants, those at the bottom of the pyramid, find themselves unable to recruit enough new members to recoup their initial investment, let alone make a profit.

The cost of falling prey to these schemes extends far beyond the monetary losses, often inflicting stress, guilt, shame and a profound sense of failure on the victims. The manipulation often leads to significant financial risks taken by the victims, such as dipping into life savings, taking on credit card debt or even mortgaging homes to invest in the scheme. However, the damage isn't just financial. Falling victim to such schemes can be emotionally traumatic. Many victims report experiencing high levels of stress due to financial loss and debt. They often grapple with feelings of guilt and shame for having brought financial hardship upon themselves and their families. This emotional toll can strain personal relationships and lead to isolation, depression and in severe cases, even suicidal thoughts.

So, while the proposition of instant riches might be tempting, the reality is that wealth accumulation is often the result of diligent savings, sensible investments and, most importantly, time. It's important to return to a fundamental truth: there is no substitute for hard work when it comes to achieving financial independence. While get-rich-quick schemes may promise a shortcut to wealth and financial independence, the reality is that they offer little more than illusions and disappointments.

Lifestyle Inflation

Lifestyle inflation is a widespread issue. Let's explore three illustrative case studies. Known globally as the "King of Pop," Michael Jackson, whose music and choreography revolutionized the entertainment industry, earned millions throughout his career. However, behind the glittering facade of fame and fortune, Jackson's financial situation was less than ideal, marked by excessive spending and enormous debt. Jackson's most extravagant investment was his 2,700-acre property, known as Neverland Ranch, a fantastical homage to the Peter Pan story. With its private amusement park, zoo and movie theater, the property was a child's dream brought to life. The maintenance of Neverland, coupled with the costs of the exotic animals, staff and utilities, reportedly cost Jackson millions annually.

In addition to his lavish real estate purchases, Jackson was known for his excessive personal spending. He underwent numerous expensive cosmetic surgery procedures, maintained an extensive staff and even adopted a pet chimpanzee named Bubbles, which added to his rising expenses. Perhaps less well known but equally detrimental to his financial health was Jackson's passion for art and antiquities. He owned an extensive art collection, with pieces ranging from contemporary art to statues and other historical artifacts, many of which came with hefty price tags. Despite earning an estimated $500 million to $1 billion throughout his career, Jackson was reportedly in debt to the tune of $400 million by the time of his death in 2009.

Nicolas Cage, the charismatic and versatile actor, is no stranger to the silver screen's highs and lows, both in his career and his personal finances. Cage, who has given memorable performances in a variety of films and won an Academy Award for his role in *Leaving Las Vegas*, earned an impressive $150 million between 1996 and 2011. However, despite this substantial fortune, he fell into serious financial trouble due to unchecked lifestyle inflation and extravagant spending.

Cage's buying habits reflected a penchant for the unusual and expensive. His real estate portfolio included not just homes in popular celebrity locations like Hollywood and Malibu, but also a castle in Germany, a haunted mansion in New Orleans and an island in the Bahamas. These properties, while grandiose, came with equally grand costs for maintenance, taxes and staffing. But Cage's spending did not stop at real estate. His eclectic taste extended to rare artifacts, including a dinosaur skull purchased for more than $300,000, shrunken pygmy heads and a collection of rare comic books. Additionally, Cage maintained a private zoo of exotic pets, including snakes and a crocodile, adding to his towering expenses. However, the upkeep of such a lavish lifestyle proved to be unsustainable. When Cage encountered issues with the Internal Revenue Service (IRS) over unpaid taxes amounting to millions of dollars, he was forced to start selling off his assets. The selling process was painful and often resulted in selling properties at a loss, exacerbating his financial predicament.

Mike Tyson, renowned for his ferocity in the boxing ring and recognized as the undisputed heavyweight champion, experienced a financial fall as dramatic as his rise in the sport. Despite earning a staggering $300 million over his boxing career, Tyson filed for bankruptcy in 2003. Tyson's spending was as legendary as his boxing prowess. Known for his fondness for extravagance, he purchased a $6.3 million mansion, which was equipped with gold-plated furnishings, an indoor pool and waterfall, and multiple cages for his pet tigers.

The spending didn't stop at his residence; Tyson's lifestyle included custom-made jewelry, high-end clothes and extravagant parties that cost thousands of dollars. One of his most notorious purchases was a $2 million bathtub that was a Christmas gift for his first wife, Robin Givens. Additionally, his love for exotic animals led him to buy Siberian tigers, each costing around $70,000, not including the astronomical food and care costs associated with these large creatures. Tyson's spending was further compounded by his legal troubles and personal issues. Convicted of rape in 1992, Tyson spent three years in prison, which halted his lucrative boxing career.

After his release, he struggled to regain his previous form and high income. Tyson also found himself in a web of debts, including back taxes and settlement costs from various lawsuits. When he declared bankruptcy in 2003, he was reported to be $23 million in debt.

As our income grows, it's a common tendency to upgrade our lifestyle accordingly. This phenomenon, known as lifestyle inflation—an increase in spending as one's income increases—can pose a significant obstacle to achieving financial independence. From moving into a bigger house to driving a more luxurious car, eating at more expensive restaurants or taking fancier vacations, these spending habits inflate your cost of living and consequently, destroy your capacity to save and invest. Each additional dollar spent on upgrading our lifestyle is a dollar not saved, invested or used to pay down debt. While we may be able to enjoy more luxuries and comfort in the present, these decisions can substantially delay, or eliminate, our progress toward financial independence and retirement. No matter how high the income, extravagant and uncontrolled spending will lead to financial ruin.

Debt Traps

Henry, a single father of two, faced an unexpected car repair bill. Short on cash and with a week to go until payday, he took out a small payday loan. He believed it was a one-time solution, but when payday arrived, he found he didn't have enough to cover both the loan and his living expenses. Henry began taking out new payday loans to pay off the old ones, entering a vicious cycle of debt that he struggled to escape.

The image of a payday loan often comes cloaked in friendly advertising, suggesting a quick and easy solution to unexpected financial emergencies. However, beneath this facade lies a financial trap that can turn a short-term crisis into a long-term debt nightmare. Payday loans are small, short-term unsecured loans that are usually tied to the borrower's payday, hence the name. They're often marketed as a convenient way to cover unexpected expenses or bridge a short-term cash crunch until the next paycheck arrives. The appeal of payday loans comes from their perceived accessibility, as they often require minimal credit checks, making them attractive to individuals with poor credit scores or those who need immediate access to funds.

Despite their small amounts, payday loans carry staggering interest rates. It's not uncommon for these loans to have an annual percentage rate (APR) of 400% or even higher. For context, credit cards, often considered high-interest debt, typically have an APR between 15% and 30%. The real danger of payday loans comes into play when borrowers cannot repay the loan plus the high-interest charge by their next payday. This could be due to the size of the repayment taking up a large chunk of their next paycheck, or because of ongoing financial difficulties that led them to seek a payday loan in the first place. If they can't repay, they might roll the debt into a new payday loan, incurring more fees and interest, and kick-starting a vicious cycle of debt.

After losing his job, Dan turned to high-interest personal loans to cover his bills. While it helped him in the short term, the monthly repayments quickly became overwhelming due to the exorbitant interest rates. The loans that were supposed to be a lifeline ended up dragging him further into financial turmoil.

The world of high-interest loans can be a minefield of financial jargon and complex terms, but understanding their mechanics is essential in grasping their potential perils. The APR of a loan is the total cost of borrowing money per year. It includes both the interest rate and any associated fees, providing a more accurate picture of what the loan will actually cost. High-interest loans typically have high APRs, which means the cost of borrowing is significantly more expensive. Compounding is the process by which interest is added to the principal (the original amount borrowed) and then additional interest is charged on this new, larger amount. This is why debts can grow rapidly and become unmanageable, especially with high-interest loans with an already-steep interest rate. For example, a $10,000 loan with an APR of 20% would grow to $12,000 after a year if the interest is compounded annually.

Some high-interest loans, like payday loans, are structured in a way that encourages or even requires borrowers to "roll over" their debt into a new loan if they're unable to pay by the due date. While this may provide temporary relief, it often comes with additional fees and a higher balance due, exacerbating the borrower's financial situation. When individuals resort to high-interest loans, it's often because they're already facing financial strain. The additional pressure of repaying these costly loans can lead to a cycle of debt. In other words, individuals take out new loans to repay old ones and each time the amount owed increases, leading to an escalating spiral of debt.

Emily, a recent college graduate, received her first credit card. At first, it was an exciting novelty and she used it responsibly. But over time, she began to treat her credit limit as an extension of her income, racking up balances on clothes, dinners out and vacations. She was making only the minimum payments each month, unaware of how quickly interest was accruing. In a few short years, Emily found herself buried in credit card debt that dwarfed her initial spending. With their high interest, if you carry a balance month to month, the interest can quickly add up, making it harder to pay off your debt. Credit card debt can impact your credit score, a crucial factor that lenders consider when you apply for loans or other forms of credit. High credit card balances can increase your credit utilization rate, which is the percentage of your total available credit that you're using. A high utilization rate can lower your credit score. Additionally, late payments on your credit cards will also negatively impact your credit score. Similar to payday loans, mismanagement of credit cards can also lead to a cycle of debt. If you continuously add to your card balance and only make minimum payments, your debt could keep growing.

The convenience of credit cards can be a double-edged sword. While they offer immediate access to funds and the ability to pay for goods and services virtually anywhere, misuse of credit cards can lead to spiraling debt and financial distress. Credit cards offer the ability to purchase now and pay later, which can sometimes create an illusion of affordability. If a person sees a high-priced item they want, a credit card allows them to purchase it immediately, even if they don't have the funds in their bank account. However, this can lead to accumulating debt if the cardholder is unable to pay off the balance in full by the due date. Credit card companies usually offer the option to make a minimum payment on your card balance each month. While this might seem like a beneficial feature, only making the minimum payment can prolong your debt and accrue substantial interest over time. That's because any remaining balance after the minimum payment is subject to interest charges, which are then added to your total balance.

In conclusion, excessive debt can be a significant roadblock on the path to financial independence. The burden of owing money not only restricts your current financial capability but also undermines your financial future. It's crucial to manage and control debt responsibly. Avoid high-interest debt whenever possible and aim to pay off existing debt as quickly as you can. The path to financial independence becomes much more straightforward and achievable when you're not burdened by carrying the heavy load of excessive debt.

Chapter 4

STEP-BY-STEP GUIDE TO F.I.R.E.

Now that we've gained insights into some common financial missteps to steer clear of, let's shift our focus to things we should prioritize. A frequent question about F.I.R.E. is, "I have [insert number] dollars, how should I best spend it?" If your objective is to achieve early retirement, I am here to chart a systematic, step-by-step guide to prioritizing your financial allocations. For ease of understanding, I have segregated this journey into ten unique stages, starting with Stage One. You can liken it to advancing through different stages in a video game. Typically, each stage paves the way for the succeeding one, although the order is not strictly linear.

While the guide predominantly caters to individuals residing in the United States, it also holds relevance for individuals across the globe. The specific financial tools and insurance plans might vary, but the underlying principles remain constant. If you're already well versed in the basics of personal finance, this guide will serve as a constructive reinforcement of your existing knowledge. I highly recommend reading all ten stages to gain a holistic view before you commit to any decisions.

Stage One: Current Financial Health

The inception of your journey toward financial independence is predicated on comprehending your present financial landscape and this stage is designed to assist you. It's vital to understand your current standing before you map a trajectory toward your desired financial destination.

Asset inventory

Your first task is taking stock of all your assets. Assets encompass a broad spectrum, including cash; savings and checking accounts; retirement funds like 401(k)s and individual retirement accounts (IRAs); investments such as stocks, bonds or mutual funds; real estate; and other valuable assets like cars, high-end jewelry or collectibles.

First, document all your liquid assets, alternatively referred to as cash and cash equivalents. This typically comprises funds in your checking and savings accounts, physical cash on hand and also assets that can be quickly liquidated, like money market funds and short-term government bonds.

Retirement accounts form a crucial segment of your asset inventory. This category includes 401(k)s, various forms of IRAs (traditional, Roth, SEP, SIMPLE), 403(b)s, Thrift Savings Plans and other specialized retirement savings accounts. Although these are typically geared for long-term accumulation, they significantly contribute to your overall financial health.

Following this, assess your investment portfolio. This consists of your holdings in stocks, bonds, mutual funds, exchange-traded funds (ETFs) and other securities in brokerage accounts. Additionally, you should include investments in private entities, equity in startups or contributions to venture capital funds.

Real estate also commands a significant presence in your asset inventory. This could range from your primary residence to rental properties, vacation homes or undeveloped land. It's crucial to estimate their worth based on the current market value, rather than the price at which you purchased the property.

Vehicles such as cars, motorcycles, boats, recreational vehicles and others form part of your valuable assets and should be accounted for in your inventory. Use their current market value for this appraisal.

Additionally, any valuable personal belongings such as jewelry, antiques, artwork, premium electronics, musical instruments or other collectibles should be recorded.

Business ownership or partial ownership also constitutes a notable asset. Appraising the value of a business can be intricate, entailing considerations like current profits, growth prospects and market conditions.

Other assets might comprise loans you've granted to others, due tax refunds, security deposits, prepaid expenses or the cash value of life insurance policies.

This exercise is about compiling a comprehensive list of everything valuable you own. It's the preliminary phase of understanding your financial landscape, offering a clear view of your available resources.

Ensure you update your asset inventory on a regular basis as the value of these assets can fluctuate over time. Maintaining an accurate and up-to-date asset inventory will guide you in making informed decisions about your financial future. Plus, having all this information aggregated will also prove beneficial in emergency situations, like sudden illness or natural disasters.

While developing your asset inventory, it's essential to be meticulous and realistic about the value of your assets. This process will offer you a transparent understanding of your possessions, which is the initial stride toward attaining financial independence.

Liability analysis

Moving beyond assets, it becomes crucial to thoroughly evaluate your liabilities. Liabilities encompass an array of financial obligations such as mortgages, student loans, credit card debts, auto loans, personal loans or any other form of indebtedness. The objective here is to fully comprehend the magnitude of your obligations, the respective recipients, the interest rates each debt carries and the associated repayment schedules. While assets denote ownership, liabilities signify what you owe. The procedure of liability analysis involves the understanding and quantification of your financial commitments. Below is how you can conduct a comprehensive liability analysis.

Begin with the most common form of long-term liability, a mortgage. If you are responsible for one or multiple mortgages, delineate each one individually, detailing the outstanding principal amount, the rate of interest and the remaining term.

Next, address any student loans you have. Much like with mortgages, provide the details of the outstanding balance, the interest rate and the remaining term for each loan. If your student loans are part of an income-based repayment or another non-standard repayment scheme, indicate that specifically.

Credit card debt is another prevalent form of liability. Catalog each credit card separately, accompanied by the outstanding balance and the rate of interest. This information will guide you in prioritizing your repayments, as you'll generally aim to settle debts with the highest interest rates first.

If your vehicle was financed, account for it as another liability. Include details about the outstanding principal, the interest rate and the remaining term of your auto loan(s), as you did for mortgages and student loans.

Personal loans, which are commonly utilized for purposes such as home improvements or debt consolidation, should also be incorporated in your liability analysis. Include specifics about the outstanding balance, interest rate and terms.

If you have a line of credit, such as a home equity line of credit (HELOC), incorporate it in your liability analysis. Note the total credit limit, the current balance and the interest rate.

Do not overlook any other debts that you owe, ranging from medical debts, IRS or other tax debts, payday loans or money owed to friends or family.

Bear in mind that the goal of the liability analysis is not to create stress or anxiety concerning your financial obligations. Instead, its purpose is to provide a crystal-clear understanding of your financial commitments, enabling you to devise an effective plan to manage them.

By explicitly outlining your liabilities, you can formulate strategies to diminish your debts, thus enhancing your net worth and propelling you closer to your financial aspirations. Being cognizant of the specifics, like the interest rates and terms of your debts, can guide you in making informed decisions about which debts to prioritize and how to evade accumulating un-necessary debt in the future.

Net worth calculation

When you've outlined your assets and liabilities, calculating your net worth is the next logical step. Your net worth is the difference between what you own (assets) and what you owe (liabilities). It's a snapshot of your financial health at a particular moment in time and represents the value of what you own minus the value of what you owe. Here's how you can calculate it:

Add up all the assets you've identified in your asset inventory.

Next, add up all your liabilities, or what you owe.

Finally, subtract your total liabilities from your total assets. The resulting number is your net worth.

Net Worth = Total Assets - Total Liabilities

Bear in mind that each individual's financial journey is distinctive and unique. If you find your net worth landing in negative territory, it's not a cause for alarm. It's quite common for young adults or those in the early stages of their career to exhibit a negative net worth due to burdens such as student loans or other forms of debt. The primary objective should be to concentrate on measures that can enhance your net worth in the long run, like debt reduction and escalating your savings and investments.

Regularly revisit your net worth calculation. It isn't a one-off task; rather, it should be routinely updated and tracked as a part of your financial journey. By consistently keeping tabs on your net worth, you get to appreciate your financial growth, comprehend the consequences of your financial decisions and modify your strategies as required.

Income and expense tracking

Grasping your monthly cash flow is of paramount importance in your financial journey. Start by documenting all your income sources, encompassing more than just your primary job. Include your salary, additional gigs, rental revenue, dividends, interest and any other income streams. Remember to distinguish between regular sources of income (like a monthly salary) and irregular ones (like sporadic freelance work). This distinction aids in tailoring your budget to reflect the variability of your income.

Outline all your expenses. Categorize these into fixed and variable costs. Fixed costs remain relatively constant month-on-month, like mortgage or car loan repayments. Conversely, variable costs are based on consumption or usage and include items such as groceries, fuel and leisure expenses. Categorizing these expenses into "necessities" and "desires" can prove beneficial. "Necessities" are indispensable for survival or contractually obligated (such as mortgage, utilities, debt repayments, etc.). In contrast, "desires" refer to discretionary spending, like dining out, holidays or shopping sprees.

Transition into tracking all your income and expenses diligently. Employ a method that suits your comfort, whether that's a spreadsheet, a budgeting application or even a straightforward notebook. Chronicle every cent that is earned or spent. This habitual practice provides a comprehensive understanding of your money's origins and its allocation.

On a monthly basis, scrutinize your income and expenses. Investigate patterns. Are there specific areas where you routinely overspend? Could you pare down or even eliminate certain expenses? Tweak your spending habits as necessary to resonate with your financial aspirations. Although the process of tracking income and expenses may initially seem labor intensive, it's an integral step toward gaining financial literacy. It imparts a thorough understanding of your spending habits, aids in establishing a pragmatic budget and empowers you to make well-informed decisions about your financial future.

Create a budget

Budgeting, a term often overlooked or misconstrued, stands at the heart of our financial well-being. Without it, we are metaphorically sailing in the dark, devoid of clear insight into our financial standing. The journey toward financial independence and early retirement demands comprehensive planning and, above all, the self-control to stick to that plan. Think of a budget as the financial counterpart of a map and compass to help navigate through unfamiliar landscapes. To make do without a budget isn't impossible, but it undeniably complicates the journey, increasing the risk of pitfalls such as spiraling into overwhelming debt or being ill equipped for financial emergencies.

So, what does budgeting truly mean? At its core, a budget is a meticulously crafted financial plan that outlines your income and expenditures over a specific period, commonly a month. It acts as an assurance that you always have sufficient funds for your necessities and the things that matter to you. Abiding by a budget or spending blueprint not only prevents debt but also aids in eliminating existing debt.

You've already pinpointed and classified your income and expenses in earlier stages. The next step involves subtracting your total expenses from your total income. A positive result indicates that your earnings exceed your spending, an optimal scenario. Conversely, a negative number reveals that your spending surpasses your income, a red flag necessitating cutbacks.

Utilizing the information gleaned from your income and expenses, tailor a budget that resonates with your requirements. Budgets can be designed on a weekly, biweekly or monthly basis, contingent on your personal choice and income regularity.

Assign your income among necessities, desires, savings and debt repayment. A widespread approach is the 50/30/20 rule, allocating 50% of income to necessities, 30% to desires and 20% to savings and debt repayment. A higher allocation to savings expedites retirement. To retire as rapidly as possible, let's rearrange the traditional allocation to 70% for savings, 20% for necessities and 10% for desires. There are a number of ways to reduce expenditure on necessities, which you'll start to address in Stage Two (page 72).

The most challenging aspect of budgeting is adherence because it demands discipline and a profound commitment to accomplishing your financial objectives. Regularly monitor your spending and juxtapose it with your budget. Persistent overspending in specific categories mandates a revision of your budget or spending habits.

Remember, your budget isn't a rigid blueprint. As life evolves, be it a new job, a salary increment, a new addition to your family or new financial objectives, your budget should mirror these changes. Periodically review and amend your budget to account for these fluctuations.

A budget isn't designed to constrict your spending. Instead, view it as a tool empowering you to spend freely, sans worry or guilt, safe in the knowledge that you're living within your means and marching toward your financial goals.

Stage Two: Living Expenses

Stage Two underscores the importance of addressing your fundamental living expenses. This phase is dedicated to guaranteeing that your core necessities are adequately met, fostering a secure and comfortable living environment devoid of financial anxiety.

Pay off housing and key utilities

Attend to all your housing-related expenses. For tenants, this includes the punctual payment of rent each month. For homeowners keep up with mortgage payments, encompassing principal, interest, taxes and insurance. Core utilities consist of electricity, heating or cooling costs, water and waste disposal services. It's of paramount importance to allocate funds for these expenses in your budget and settle them promptly to prevent late fees, penalties or service discontinuation.

Purchase food and household essentials

Budget for food and grocery items. Preparing meals and crafting shopping lists can aid in conserving money and helping you steer clear of unwarranted expenditure. Also account for other household essentials like cleaning materials and personal care products in your budget. Pet owners should also incorporate their pets' food and care requirements into the grocery budget.

Handle income-generating expenditure

Manage costs associated with your capacity to generate income. This might involve transportation expenses such as car payments, fuel, maintenance, insurance or public transportation costs. If your work depends on internet access, your internet service bill falls within this category. For freelancers or business owners, costs for software, hardware and other job-related tools should also be considered.

Account for health care expenses

Health care expenses can fluctuate substantially based on your health condition, insurance coverage and geographic location. Budget for regular health care costs, encompassing health insurance premiums, out-of-pocket charges for doctor appointments, medications and preventive care. It's crucial to prepare for unanticipated health care costs as well, such as emergency room visits or sudden health complications.

Fulfill minimum payments on debts and loans

Make regular payments on credit cards, student loans, car loans or personal loans. Failing to make these payments can result in late fees, increased interest rates and detrimental effects on your credit score. While fulfilling minimum payments is necessary, it's equally important to strive toward paying more than the minimum, especially on high-interest debts, to expedite their clearance. Always keep track of the interest rates and terms of your loans and consider refinancing options when beneficial.

Stage Three: Emergency Fund and Financial Optimizations

Life can be compared to a rollercoaster, filled with exhilarating highs and challenging lows. The unpredictability necessitates the creation of an emergency fund, a financial safety net designed to cushion the impact of unexpected expenses. Whether it's a sudden car breakdown, an unexpected appliance repair or an abrupt job loss, life has a way of surprising us. An emergency fund serves as your financial buffer against these unforeseen expenses, preventing them from driving you into debt or forcing you to choose between addressing the emergency or meeting your regular financial obligations.

The real charm of an emergency fund lies in the sense of financial security and peace of mind it provides. It equips you with the financial resilience to face unexpected costs without disturbing your planned budget or spiraling you into debt. Moreover, should you find yourself in a situation where you lose your job or need to take an unplanned hiatus from work, your emergency fund stands ready to cover your expenses, keeping you financially afloat until you regain your footing.

To ensure optimal use of your emergency fund, consider stashing it in a Federal Deposit Insurance Corporation (FDIC)–insured high-yield savings account. These types of savings accounts typically offer higher interest rates compared to traditional savings accounts, allowing your money to grow more effectively over time. The beauty of choosing an FDIC-insured account is the security it provides. The FDIC is an independent agency of the U.S. government designed to protect and preserve the integrity of the nation's banking system. This means that even in the unlikely event of the bank failing, your money, up to $250,000 per depositor per bank, is guaranteed safe. I personally recommend Ally Bank or American Express National Bank as they offer some of the best in class for competitive rates, low minimum deposits and no monthly fees.

Start with a small emergency fund

This initial fund should be about $1,000, or equivalent to one month of your basic living expenses, whichever is greater. This small fund provides a cushion against minor unexpected costs such as a car repair or an unplanned medical bill.

Maximize your employer-sponsored retirement match

Many employers offer a retirement savings match as part of their benefits package, typically in the form of a 401(k) match. This essentially means that your employer will contribute a certain amount to your 401(k) for every dollar that you contribute, up to a certain limit. This is effectively free money and you should take full advantage. For example, if your employer offers a 100% match up to 5% of your salary and you make $60,000 a year, you should aim to contribute at least $3,000 (which is 5% of your salary) to your 401(k). Your employer would then also contribute $3,000, effectively doubling your contribution.

Pay off high-interest debt

Pay off any debt you have that is above 10%. This generally includes things like credit cards and personal loans.

Gradually increase the fund

Next, gradually increase the fund. Aim to contribute a certain percentage of your monthly income to your emergency fund. This percentage should be based on your risk profile and how secure you feel with your job. The goal is to eventually build up an emergency fund that can cover three to six months' worth of expenses.

Maintain the fund and replenish when necessary

Once you've established your emergency fund, you need to maintain it. It's critical to avoid dipping into the fund unless it's absolutely necessary. If you do end up using some of the money, make it a priority to replenish the amount as soon as possible. This ensures your fund stays intact and ready for any future emergencies.

Review and adjust

Periodically review and adjust the size of your emergency fund. As your life circumstances change (perhaps you have a child, buy a house or experience changes in your health), your monthly expenses may increase, requiring a larger emergency fund. Regularly reviewing your fund ensures that it continues to meet your needs.

Stage Four: Reducing Debt

The burden of debt can be overwhelming, acting as a substantial obstacle to your financial well-being and creating stress. In the fourth stage of our journey toward financial independence and early retirement, I'll explain two of the most prominent strategies to efficiently tackle your debt load.

The avalanche method and the snowball method, each with its unique approach, have proven to be successful for many individuals on their journey to becoming debt-free. The method that suits you best is dependent on your personal circumstances, as well as what motivates and inspires you to stay the course.

The avalanche method is characterized by paying off debts with the highest interest rates first, potentially resulting in significant cost savings over time. On the other hand, the snowball method, which advocates for paying off smaller debts first, provides a motivational boost as you quickly see progress in your debt-reduction efforts. Regardless of the strategy you choose, the key is to select an approach that resonates with you, one you can commit to consistently, propelling you toward your ultimate goal of freeing yourself from the shackles of debt.

It's important to note that when discussing debt, we usually exclude mortgage debt because it often carries an interest rate below the "prime rate."

The prime rate, often referred to as the prime lending rate, is the interest rate that commercial banks offer to their most credit-worthy clients, who are typically large corporations. The rate is often influenced by the federal funds rate, which is the rate at which banks lend to each other for short-term loans. This prime rate is an essential interest rate that impacts various other rates for consumer loans, credit cards and adjustable-rate mortgages. It acts as a reference point for many different types of loans and credit lines.

During periods of low interest rates, often linked with a low prime rate, borrowing becomes more affordable. Such times can provide excellent opportunities for businesses to secure loans for expansion, or for individuals to incur debt for various purposes such as home improvements, educational expenses or other personal requirements.

Debt carrying an interest rate below the prime rate is not always detrimental. This is because the cost of borrowing that money is relatively low, enabling potentially profitable financial maneuvers, such as arbitrage. Arbitrage involves borrowing money at a low interest rate, such as 3%, and investing it in a venture that provides a higher return, say 5%. In this scenario, you stand to profit by the 2% difference.

However, it's crucial to remember that each investment carries risk and returns are never guaranteed. The value of investments can decrease as well as increase. Furthermore, despite the low interest rate, the debt is still a liability that must be repaid. Should your circumstances change, leaving you unable to pay back the loan, you could find yourself in a challenging financial predicament, regardless of the interest rate on your debt.

Avalanche method

The avalanche method involves focusing on debts with the highest interest rates first. Here's how it works:

1. List all your debts, from the highest interest rate to the lowest.
2. Make minimum payments on all your debts.
3. Any extra money you have goes toward the debt with the highest interest rate.
4. When the highest interest debt is paid off, move to the debt with the next highest interest rate.
5. Repeat this process until all your debts are paid off.

The advantage of the avalanche method is that it saves you the most money in the long run, as you're paying off the most expensive debts first. However, it may take a while before you start seeing progress, especially if your highest interest debt also has a high balance. Mathematically, this method is the better of the two if you're able to stick with it.

Snowball method

The snowball method involves paying off debts with the smallest balances first. Here's how it works:

1. List all your debts, from the smallest balance to the largest.
2. Make minimum payments on all your debts.

3. Any extra money you have goes toward the debt with the smallest balance.
4. When the smallest debt is paid off, move to the debt with the next smallest balance.
5. Repeat this process until all your debts are paid off.

The advantage of the snowball method is the psychological boost you get from paying off a debt in full. This can provide a sense of accomplishment and motivate you to keep going. The disadvantage of this method is you might end up paying more in interest over time compared to the avalanche method.

Stage Five: Insurance Needs

Insurance provides financial protection against unexpected events and is an integral part of a healthy financial plan. It can help protect your assets, cover medical expenses, provide for your family in the event of your death and more. Understanding your insurance needs involves assessing your risks and determining the best insurance products to mitigate those risks. While insurance is an expense that you hope you'll never need to use, having it can provide invaluable peace of mind and financial security. For those that live in the United States, you are eligible to be covered under a parent's health insurance if you're under the age of 26.

There are several types of insurance you may need to consider:

- **Health insurance:** covers medical expenses such as hospital stays, doctor visits and prescriptions.
- **Life insurance:** provides financial support to your dependents if you die.
- **Homeowner's or renter's insurance:** protects your home and personal belongings from damage or theft.
- **Auto insurance:** covers vehicle damage and liabilities if you cause an accident.
- **Disability insurance:** replaces a portion of your income if you're unable to work due to a disability.

Assess your risks

Consider your personal situation and the potential financial risks you face. For example, if you have a family that relies on your income, life insurance is a must. If you own a home, homeowner's insurance is critical to protect your asset. Your job, lifestyle, health condition and family situation all play a role in your insurance needs.

Determine the right coverage amount

The amount of coverage you need depends on various factors. For instance, your life insurance should be enough to cover your family's living expenses and pay off debts in case of your demise. Similarly, your health insurance should be sufficient to cover potential medical costs given your health condition. Car insurance is legally required for people who drive a motor vehicle in the United States.

Shop around for the best policies

Don't settle for the first policy you find. Instead, shop around, compare different policies and choose the one that provides the best coverage for your needs at an affordable price. Online comparison tools can be helpful for this process.

Open a health savings account

Health savings accounts, or HSAs, serve as an invaluable resource for managing health care costs, particularly if you're under a high-deductible health plan. Their unique attributes, including a blend of tax benefits, versatility and potential for growth, provide a practical avenue for funding medical expenses and future planning. Essentially, an HSA is a special type of savings account that allows you to allocate pre-tax dollars to cover qualified medical expenditures. Utilizing an HSA to manage deductibles, co-payments, coinsurance and other out-of-pocket costs can significantly reduce your overall health care burden. For 2023, the HSA contribution limits stand at $3,850 for self-only coverage and $7,750 for family coverage. Individuals aged 55 and above can make an additional $1,000 in catch-up contributions. To qualify for HSA contributions, you must be enrolled in an HSA-eligible health plan and should not be enrolled in Medicare or claimed as a dependent on someone else's tax return.

Let's discuss how HSAs can be advantageous:

1. **Triple tax benefits:** HSAs are often hailed for their unique "triple tax benefits." The contributions you make to an HSA are tax deductible, thereby reducing your taxable income for the year.

   - **Tax-free growth:** The funds in an HSA grow tax-free. Many HSAs even allow you to invest your contributions, much like a 401(k) or an IRA, meaning your savings can potentially grow even faster over time due to compound interest. This can help you build a substantial health care nest egg for your retirement years.

   - **Tax-free distributions:** When you withdraw money from an HSA for qualified medical expenses, the withdrawals are tax-free. The list of qualifying expenses is quite extensive, including prescription medications, doctor visits, surgeries and even dental and vision care.

2. **Rollover of unused funds:** In contrast to a flexible spending account (FSA), HSAs do not operate under a "use it or lose it" policy. Any unused funds in your HSA roll over from year to year, providing an opportunity to accumulate savings over time.

3. **Future planning:** Once you reach 65, you can use your HSA funds for any purpose, penalty-free. If the funds are utilized for non-medical expenditures, they'll be subject to your regular income tax rate.

4. **Investment opportunities:** Numerous HSA providers permit account holders to invest their HSA funds in a range of investment options, akin to a 401(k) or IRA. This offers a chance to grow the value of your HSA over time.

5. **Ownership:** HSAs are owned by the individual, not the employer. Therefore, if you transition to a new job, your HSA account stays with you, ensuring continuous coverage and savings potential.

While HSAs provide attractive tax benefits, it's crucial to be aware of potential tax penalties related to overcontributions or spending the funds on ineligible expenses.

If your contributions exceed the annual maximum limit in a particular year, you could be hit with a 6% excise tax on the excess amount. This tax penalty applies not only in the year you contributed too much, but also in each subsequent year that the surplus amount and its earnings remain in the account. Moreover, the excess contribution is deemed taxable income. However, if you rectify the overcontribution before the tax filing deadline for that year, you can generally dodge both income tax and the excise tax for that year.

Should you withdraw HSA funds for nonqualified expenses, a substantial tax penalty awaits. If you're under the age of 65, you'll face a 20% penalty, plus any related income taxes on the withdrawn amount. However, if you're 65 or older, you're allowed to spend HSA funds on ineligible expenses without incurring a penalty, though you'll still be responsible for paying income taxes.

If your HSA-eligible health plan doesn't cover you for the entire year, you might only be able to contribute a portion of the full allowable amount. That said, if you're covered on December 1 of the relevant year, you may still be able to contribute the maximum annual amount.

To work out your pro-rated contribution limit, calculate the number of months you were enrolled in an HSA-eligible health plan as of the first day of the month, divide this figure by 12 and then multiply the resulting number by the total amount you could contribute if you were eligible for the entire year. Generally, you have until the tax filing deadline to make contributions to an HSA.

Last, don't forget to invest the money in your HSA account. Choose a low-cost S&P 500 index fund like $VOO or the closest equivalent (see more on page 90 about this). Typically, HSA accounts require some sort of minimum be available in cash to cover health care expenses and will sell off your investments if your account ever gets below this required minimum balance.

Stage Six: IRA Investing

Types of IRAs

There are two primary types of IRAs, Roth IRAs and traditional IRAs. While both are designed to help you save for retirement, each has its unique characteristics, benefits and drawbacks. Understanding these can help you make an informed choice about where to put your retirement savings. For our international readers, the gist of this and the next three stages is to max out your tax-advantaged accounts related to retirement and education.

Traditional IRA

A traditional IRA is a type of retirement account that provides tax advantages for retirement savings in the United States. Contributions to a Traditional IRA are often tax deductible, meaning they reduce your taxable income for the year in which you make the contribution. The funds in the account then grow, tax-deferred. When you withdraw the money in retirement, it is taxed as ordinary income.

Pros of traditional IRA

- **Tax deductions:** You get an immediate tax break because contributions are often made with pre-tax dollars, though the deduction phases out at higher income levels.
- **Deferred taxes:** The investment growth in a traditional IRA is tax deferred, meaning you won't pay taxes on dividends, interest or capital gains until you start making withdrawals.

Cons of traditional IRA

- **Required minimum distributions (RMDs):** Starting at age 73, the IRS mandates that you begin taking RMDs from your traditional IRA, regardless of whether you need the money.
- **Penalty for early withdrawal:** With some exceptions, if you withdraw funds from your traditional IRA before age 59½, you'll pay a 10% early withdrawal penalty plus income tax on the amount you withdraw.

Roth IRA

Unlike a traditional IRA, contributions to a Roth IRA are made with after-tax dollars, meaning you pay tax on the money before you invest it. The advantage is that you won't owe any tax on the funds when you withdraw them in retirement, as long as you meet certain conditions. Additionally, your investments grow tax-free and there are no RMDs.

Pros of Roth IRA

- **Tax-free withdrawals**: Because you fund a Roth IRA with after-tax dollars, your money grows tax-free, and you won't owe taxes on withdrawals in retirement, provided you meet the qualifications.

- **No RMDs**: Unlike traditional IRAs, Roth IRAs don't require you to start taking withdrawals at a certain age, which can provide more flexibility in managing your income and taxes in retirement.

Cons of Roth IRA

- **Income limitations**: Roth IRAs come with income restrictions. If you earn above a certain threshold, your ability to contribute to a Roth IRA is reduced or eliminated altogether.

- **No immediate tax benefit**: Because Roth IRA contributions are made with after-tax dollars, you won't receive an immediate tax deduction.

For the 2023 tax year, the total annual contribution limits across all your traditional and Roth IRAs have been set at $6,500 for individuals under 50 and $7,500 for those who are 50 or older. Please note that these limits encompass both types of accounts cumulatively; you can't contribute the maximum amount to each type of IRA separately. Depending on your level of income, you may find that your actual contribution limits are lower than these thresholds.

Max out your Roth IRA

If you are below the income limits for a Roth IRA, max out your contributions. The income limits for 2023 are less than $153,000 for single tax filers, and less than $228,000 for those married and filing jointly.

Max out your traditional IRA

If you are over the income limits for a Roth IRA, max out contributions to a traditional IRA.

Simplified Employee Pension (SEP) IRA

This is a retirement savings account for small business owners and the self-employed. It allows for higher contribution limits than a traditional or Roth IRA.

Invest the money in your IRA

While this step might seem obvious, I've heard one too many stories of people who have put money into their IRA but failed to actually invest in anything. Buy $VOO or the closest equivalent S&P 500 fund. This same advice applies to any type of investment account you might have. Always remember to invest the money you have deposited in your investment accounts; don't let your money sit there without working for you.

What online brokerage I use

Assuming you don't already have a brokerage account provided by your employer, I recommend you use Fidelity. I personally use them for all my retirement-related accounts and personal retail brokerage accounts. They offer the best combination of features, low to nonexistent fees and ease of use. As one of the leading financial institutions of the world, they are known for their technological innovation and robust costumer support. Most online brokerages are decent these days, but you can't go wrong with Fidelity.com.

You can set up deposits via two different methods: direct deposit of a paycheck, or recurring transfers from a bank account. You can set up the direct deposit of a paycheck by contacting the HR department of your company. For recurring bank transfers, you can generally set that up either at your bank's website or by logging in to Fidelity.

Once you have an account at Fidelity, you have the option to establish an automated investment plan within your brokerage, retirement, 529 savings or other qualified retail accounts. This allows for automatic investments into funds you currently hold, utilizing either the existing cash within the account or funds from a linked bank account. You can set this up via the Fidelity website.

Stage Seven: 401(k) Investing

The 401(k) plan is a retirement savings strategy utilized by many employers in the United States to provide their workers with tax advantages while they save for retirement. Participants of the 401(k) plan consent to a fraction of their income being directly transferred into an investment account each time they receive their paycheck. To encourage participation, many employers match a certain portion of these contributions. The participants can select from a variety of investment options, typically mutual funds. Similar to IRAs, they also come in the traditional and Roth varieties, along with contribution limits per year and various withdrawal rules.

Depending on the plan your employer provides, you might be limited in your investment selections. Most plans offer some sort of target retirement date choice as an investment option and the further out the date the more aggressive the investment style will be. If there is an investment option that mirrors the S&P 500, or is reasonably close, pick that one. Contact HR or Employee Benefits at your company to set one up.

Traditional 401(k)

A traditional 401(k) plan allows employees to contribute a portion of their pre-tax earnings, which means that contributions are made from an employee's gross income before any income tax is levied on it. This feature of a traditional 401(k) has a twofold advantage. First, it provides an immediate tax relief because the contributions reduce the taxable income for the current year. For instance, if you earn $100,000 in a year and contribute $15,000 to your 401(k), you will only be taxed on $85,000. This effectively acts as a tax deduction and can significantly lower your tax bill for the contribution year.

Second, the money deposited in the 401(k), along with any returns generated from its investment, grows tax deferred. This means that any capital gains or dividends from the investments within the 401(k) are not subject to taxes as long as they remain in the account. This tax-deferred growth can have a considerable impact on the size of your retirement nest egg, as the money that would otherwise go to taxes instead remains in your account, compounding and growing over time. However, it's important to understand that the tax relief offered by a traditional 401(k) is temporary. When you withdraw the funds during retirement, income taxes will be due on the withdrawals. This implies that while you can defer taxes, you can't escape them completely.

Roth 401(k)

Contributions to a Roth 401(k) are subtracted from your net income, which is your pay after income tax deductions. Thus, there are no tax deductions for the year of contribution. However, when you retire and start withdrawing money from the plan, these withdrawals are not subject to any additional taxes.

It is worth noting that while contributions to a Roth 401(k) are made with post-tax income, early withdrawals before the age of 59½ might lead to tax penalties.

Unfortunately, not all employers provide a Roth account option. If a Roth option is available, you can choose to contribute to either a traditional 401(k) or a Roth 401(k), or even both, subject to the annual contribution limit.

The maximum amount you can contribute to a 401(k) varies per year. As of 2023, it was $22,500. If you are 50 or older, you can contribute an additional catch-up contribution of $7,500 in 2023, resulting in a total contribution limit of $30,000 for 2023. Note that there are restrictions on the matching contribution by the employer. The total contribution by both the employee and employer cannot surpass $66,000 in 2023. If you're over 50, the limit increases to $73,500 in 2023. Employer contributions are also limited to 25% of an employee's salary.

Stage Eight: Tax-Advantaged Accounts

Employee stock purchase plans (ESPPs), 529 plans and Cover-dell education savings accounts (ESAs) offer unique benefits and considerations for individuals. ESPPs offer the potential for significant financial gains if the company performs well, while 529 plans and ESAs offer tax-advantaged ways to save for educational expenses. By understanding the nuances of these plans, you can leverage them effectively to meet your financial goals.

ESPPs

Many companies offer ESPPs, a unique financial vehicle, as part of their comprehensive benefits package. This employer-sponsored program enables participating employees to buy shares of the company at a preferential price, usually with a significant discount off the current market price.

These plans function through payroll deductions; a predeter-mined portion of the employee's salary is set aside throughout an offering period. This period typically spans several months, during which the accumulated funds are held in anticipation of the purchase period. When the purchase period arrives, the company takes the collected funds and purchases company shares on behalf of the employees participating in the plan. The real highlight of this program is the discount on the shares, typically ranging from 10% to 15% less than the prevailing market price. This gives employees an immediate return on their investment, assuming the stock price does not drastically decline immediately after the purchase.

ESPPs can represent a fantastic investment opportunity, particularly if the company's stock maintains a strong performance trajectory. But, like all investments, they come with their share of risk. A common pitfall is the potential for overexposure to company stock, which could lead to substantial financial risk should the company's fortunes decline or the overall market suffers a downturn.

As a rule of thumb, it's critical not to put all your eggs in one basket, and this is especially true with ESPPs. Diversifying your portfolio helps safeguard against fluctuations in a single stock or sector. In practical terms, it's typically a good strategy to sell the company stock as soon as the plan's rules permit and reinvest that capital in a diversified investment, like an S&P 500 index fund with low fees such as $VOO.

529 plans

Among the multitude of strategies for saving and investing toward future goals, Section 529 of the Internal Revenue Code provides a valuable tax-advantaged tool explicitly designed to stimulate saving for forthcoming educational expenses. Named in honor of this section, 529 plans have become instrumental for families nationwide to plan for the increasing costs of education. What makes these 529 plans particularly enticing is their tax-free nature at both federal and, often, state levels. This applies as long as the funds withdrawn from these plans are used for eligible educational expenditures. The implications of such tax advantages can result in significant savings over time, facilitating the more manageable bearing of educational costs. Within the umbrella of 529 plans, you'll encounter two distinct types: prepaid tuition plans and education savings plans. Each comes with its unique features and benefits to suit different needs and circumstances.

The prepaid tuition plans are essentially a means of hedging against future inflation in the education sector. As an account holder, you can prepay the tuition and fees at eligible institutions for the beneficiary, all at today's rates. This plan serves to "lock in" the current cost of education, providing some degree of financial predictability against the backdrop of steadily rising education costs.

On the other hand, education savings plans operate somewhat differently. Instead of prepaying tuition, this plan enables account holders to funnel money into an investment account. The funds accrued here can then be used to pay for a broad array of college expenses for the beneficiary. This could range from tuition fees to room and board, textbooks and even costs associated with K–12 education. However, there is an element of risk to consider with education savings plans. Unlike their prepaid counterparts, these plans aren't state guaranteed. Therefore, the account balance and its potential growth are subject to the performance of the chosen investments, which can fluctuate in line with market conditions.

Coverdell ESAs

An alternative to 529 plans is the Coverdell ESA, also colloquially known as an "education IRA." Like its 529 counterparts, a Coverdell ESA is a tax-advantaged investment account. Its purpose aligns closely with that of 529 plans, to incentivize the accumulation of savings to cover forthcoming education costs. The Coverdell ESA distinguishes itself in its flexibility of usage. Unlike a 529 plan, which primarily targets post-secondary education expenses, a Coverdell ESA extends its reach to include costs associated with any level of education. This encompasses everything from primary and secondary school expenses to higher education costs.

Despite the undeniable tax advantages associated with a Coverdell ESA, the contributions made to this account are not tax deductible. This means you can't reduce your taxable income in the year you make the contribution. However, the silver lining lies in the fact that the funds in a Coverdell ESA grow tax-free until the time of distribution. This tax-free growth can make a significant impact on the amount available when it's time for the beneficiary to start their education journey. Furthermore, the beneficiary is exempt from paying tax upon withdrawal, as long as the funds are used for qualified education expenses.

The Coverdell ESA does come with a limitation on the maximum annual contribution per beneficiary. As it stands, the cap is set at $2,000 per year for each beneficiary. Despite this limitation, the tax-free growth of these contributions and their applicability toward educational costs at any level make Coverdell ESAs an appealing option for many families.

Stage Nine: Mega Backdoor Roth IRA

A "mega backdoor Roth IRA" is not an official type of retirement account but rather a financial strategy that allows individuals to contribute more money to a Roth IRA than the traditional annual limit. This strategy leverages the rules concerning after-tax contributions and Roth conversions in employer-sponsored retirement plans such as 401(k)s.

Traditional direct contributions to a Roth IRA are limited based on income. However, the mega backdoor Roth IRA strategy allows you to potentially contribute tens of thousands more to your Roth IRA every year, depending on your 401(k) plan rules and IRS limits.

To make use of a mega backdoor Roth, you first need to have a 401(k) plan that allows after-tax contributions over and above the standard deferral limit and also permits in-service withdrawals or conversions. The contribution limit for 401(k) plans, including both employee and employer contributions, was $66,000 in 2023, or $73,500 for those 50 or older. This limit is significantly higher than the standard employee contribution limit of $22,500 ($30,000 for those 50 or older), leaving room for after-tax contributions.

Here's how it works:

- Maximize your standard pre-tax or Roth 401(k) contributions (which is $22,500 or $26,000 if 50 or older in 2023).

- Accept the employer (company) contribution, which is usually a match up to a certain percentage.

- Make after-tax contributions to your 401(k), up to the total limit of $66,000 (or $73,500 for those aged 50 or older).

- Finally, roll over these after-tax contributions into a Roth IRA, where they can grow tax-free and be withdrawn tax-free in retirement.

Keep in mind the normal contribution limits to a Roth IRA are $6,500 ($7,500 if you're age 50 or older). This approach allows you to contribute significantly more, potentially tenfold the usual amount, and is entirely legal.

The mega backdoor Roth IRA is a powerful strategy for boosting your tax-free retirement savings, but it isn't right for everyone and it does come with some complexities. Here are a few things to keep in mind:

- Not all 401(k) plans allow after-tax contributions or in-service distributions, both of which are necessary for this strategy. This mostly depends on your company's policies.

- If your plan does allow after-tax contributions but not in-service distributions, you may still be able to use this strategy when you leave your job or retire, but you'll miss out on the tax-free growth in the meantime.

- There can be significant tax implications if you have pre-tax funds in your 401(k) or a traditional IRA, due to the pro-rata rule. This rule requires that when you convert funds to a Roth IRA, a portion of the conversion is considered pre-tax and a portion after-tax, based on the total balance of all your pre-tax accounts. This could result in unexpected tax liabilities.

Stage Ten: Taxable Investment Account and Paying Off Low-Interest Debt

Upon successfully navigating through the previous stages and finding yourself with additional funds to invest, it's time to start investing in a non-retirement, taxable investment brokerage account and consider paying off your low-interest debt. When your total investments hit your F.I.R.E. target number so you can sustain your living costs with the 4% rule, you will have completed Stage Ten.

Open a taxable investment account

Distinct from retirement accounts, which generally impose contribution limits and levy penalties for early withdrawals, taxable accounts offer a degree of flexibility that's unmatched. They do not cap your contributions and offer the freedom to withdraw funds at any time, sans penalties. This feature is particularly advantageous for those seeking to retire early and needing access to their investments before the traditional retirement age. During this stage, your investment strategy remains consistent, focusing on low-cost, diversified investments. Continue to channel your surplus income into Vanguard's S&P 500 ETF ($VOO). As previously stated, I personally use and recommend Fidelity.

Pay off mortgage and other low-interest debt

When your investment income comfortably covers your lifestyle expenses, it may be time to consider eliminating any remaining low-interest debt, such as your mortgage. A mortgage, often referred to as "good debt," is considered beneficial due to its relatively low interest rates and potential tax advantages. However, achieving total debt freedom can create a profound sense of financial peace and security. The path to financial independence is not solely about wealth accumulation but also about the reduction of financial stress. By completely paying off your mortgage, you're effectively decreasing your regular monthly expenses. This reduction could have a meaningful impact on your financial health, especially in retirement. Less money earmarked for debt repayment translates into lower annual withdrawals from your investments.

Chapter 5

HOW TO MAXIMIZE YOUR INCOME

In this chapter, we'll embark on a deep-dive exploration of the ways to earn more. And no, I'm not talking about scratching off lottery tickets or hoping for a surprise inheritance from a distant relative. We'll go through concrete, actionable strategies that can boost your earnings in a substantial way.

Cultivating the Money Mindset

Let's start our exploration into the world of maximizing earnings, beginning at the heart of it all, your mindset. The significance of adopting a positive and forward-thinking mindset in relation to money and growth is crucial. It's the fuel that powers your decision-making process, directs your actions and, ultimately, charts the course of your financial prosperity.

Essentially, a "money mindset" is your overarching system of beliefs and attitudes toward money: your thought processes, emotional responses and management tactics concerning your finances. It's important to clarify that nurturing a positive money mindset doesn't equate to an unhealthy obsession with wealth or transforming into a miserly figure. It's more about maintaining an acute awareness of financial growth potential and possessing an upbeat, proactive attitude toward enhancing your financial health.

Combine your "money mindset" with a "growth mindset," and you've concocted a recipe for success. The concept of a growth mindset, as conceived by psychologist Carol Dweck, revolves around the belief that your capabilities and intelligence can be cultivated through dedication, industriousness and a passion for learning. When this belief system is applied to your financial journey, it implies interpreting challenges and setbacks as stepping stones for learning and growth, not overwhelming hurdles.

Consider Josh and Sarah, both recent college graduates embarking on their respective career journeys.

Josh firmly believes in the idea that intelligence and talents are innate, bestowed upon individuals at birth, much like a genetic lottery. According to his perspective, these traits are constant, unchanging, just as immutable as eye color or height. This conviction forms the bedrock of what is known as a "fixed mindset." Josh views his capacity to earn, save and grow wealth as predetermined, controlled by his current abilities and circumstances. His belief? "I am not a math person; I will never understand investments and finances."

Sarah, on the other hand, embraces a remarkably different perspective. She believes that intelligence and abilities are not fixed traits but rather attributes that can be cultivated over time through effort, persistence and a hunger for learning. Sarah embodies the growth mindset. She sees her earning potential as fluid, something she can positively influence by expanding her skills and seeking new knowledge. Her belief? "I may not understand finances yet, but I am willing to learn and improve."

Fast forward five years.

Josh, clinging to his fixed mindset, sticks with jobs he knows he can handle, avoiding risks and challenges. He limits his income potential by not seeking promotions or job changes that would require him to learn new skills. He never attempts to understand finances, investments or strategies for increasing wealth, seeing them as beyond his grasp.

On the other side, Sarah, fueled by her growth mindset, continuously strives to enhance her skills and knowledge. She constantly seeks out new challenges, undeterred by the initial difficulty or the prospect of failure. She spends time each week learning about finances, investments and wealth-creation strategies. As her understanding grows, she begins making intelligent investment choices and seeks out higher paying job opportunities that align with her developing skills.

As the years roll by, the difference in their financial situations becomes stark. Josh, with his fixed mindset, remains in his comfort zone, living from paycheck to paycheck. In contrast, Sarah's growth mindset leads her to accumulate wealth and achieve financial independence at a much younger age than most.

In the grand chessboard of life, both Josh and Sarah started at the same square, but the mindsets they adopted drastically influenced the moves they made and the subsequent squares they reached. In the context of your income and financial independence, ask yourself: "Would I rather be a Josh or a Sarah?"

In the realm of personal finance, a growth mindset can potentially revolutionize the game. How so? Simply because it empowers us to perceive challenges as platforms for growth rather than obstacles. It motivates us to interpret failure as a valuable learning opportunity rather than a terminal roadblock. Most significantly, it fosters a belief that we can enhance our financial standing, regardless of our starting point. Mistakes, failures and setbacks often carry a negative connotation. However, when viewed from a learning perspective, they can be powerful tools in our journey toward personal and financial growth. Mistakes provide an opportunity to analyze our actions, identify areas of improvement and refine our strategies accordingly.

The elegance of a growth mindset lies in its straightforwardness. It's neither a complex financial strategy nor a well-guarded secret to wealth. It's a paradigm shift that can redefine the way you approach your income. A growth mindset can turn "I can't afford this" into "How can I afford this?" It can modify "I'll never be able to earn more" into "What strategies can I implement to increase my earnings?"

Embracing a growth mindset involves acknowledging that your financial trajectory isn't predetermined. You're not fated to live from paycheck to paycheck, nor are you consigned to remain stuck in a low-paying occupation. With patience, dedication and resilience, you hold the power to enhance your financial status. A growth mindset isn't merely a theoretical notion, it's an exceptionally pragmatic, influential tool that can reshape your financial destiny. When deployed in your financial situation, a growth mindset transitions your focus from limitations to opportunities, from present conditions to future prospects. But how does this mindset influence your income? Let's dig deeper to unravel this.

Imagine finding yourself in a situation in which you feel your job doesn't compensate you adequately. With a fixed mindset, you might convince yourself that you've merely drawn the short straw, or that lucrative jobs are reserved only for the "intellectual elite" or the "privileged." Such a mindset might result in you accepting your current earnings as the pinnacle of your financial capability.

Alternatively, incorporating a growth mindset into this scenario can dramatically flip the narrative. Rather than viewing yourself as a passive spectator at the mercy of circumstance, you would scout for avenues for growth. You would strategize ways to enhance your worth within your firm or potentially look for better opportunities in other organizations. The idea of augmenting your skillset or broadening your educational qualifications might appeal to you. You would perceive your existing situation not as a dead end, but as a launchpad. This mindset can unlock pathways to higher earnings that you might have previously considered unattainable.

This paradigm shift isn't confined only to your job scenario. A growth mindset can revolutionize the way you navigate saving, investing and spending, leading to more informed choices and superior financial outcomes. It can instigate you to undertake calculated risks, discover new income streams and venture outside your comfort zone. To alter your financial trajectory, it's imperative to acknowledge that every effort bears fruit. Each stride you make, each risk you undertake and each failure you learn from incrementally steers you closer to your financial objectives. Each setback lays the foundation for a rebound and each hurdle is a stepping stone propelling you toward substantial financial success.

Now that we've understood the potency of a growth mindset, let's explore the human psyche. We'll examine a concept I prefer to term "money consciousness": the attitudes, beliefs and emotions we associate with money. Paralleling a growth mindset, your money consciousness can wield a profound influence on your income.

Our money consciousness frequently forms subconsciously, drawing inspiration from our parental influences, societal norms and personal encounters. You might recall hearing maxims like "Money doesn't grow on trees," or "We can't afford that," during your formative years. Alternatively, you might have observed the financial tribulations or triumphs of those in your immediate environment. These experiences, consciously or subconsciously, mold our money consciousness. If your upbringing instilled in you the belief that money is scant, arduous to earn or a source of stress, you're inclined to carry these beliefs into your adulthood. They can manifest as financial self-destruction, fear of prosperity or a dearth of confidence in managing money. On the other hand, if you equate money with opportunity, security and liberation, you're inclined to foster a healthier rapport with your finances.

So, what's the strategy to transform your money consciousness? The journey begins with awareness. Identify the beliefs you've harbored and question their legitimacy. Is money genuinely scarce or does it abound? Is it truly challenging to earn or are there opportunities you've yet to explore? This slight shift in perspective, though nuanced, can drastically reconfigure your financial reality.

Replace negative money convictions with encouraging affirmations. Instead of declaring "I'm always broke," try "I'm on the path to financial independence." Instead of asserting "I'll never accumulate wealth," say "My income is increasing day by day." It might feel peculiar initially, but remember, your mind wields immense power. The language you employ crafts your reality. Sculpting your money consciousness isn't a swift transformation, it will require time, endurance and relentless commitment. However, the pay-off is a harmonious relationship with money, a mindset tailored toward financial expansion and a clear trajectory to income maximization. Remember, your beliefs can architect your financial reality. Make certain they're constructing it to favor *you*.

I encourage you to reflect on your own mindset. Are there beliefs that demand reevaluating? Are there possibilities you might have disregarded? The metamorphosis of your financial fate starts with altering your mindset.

Learning Effectively

As I discussed in the introduction, I used to be the golden boy of academics throughout my school years. From kindergarten to high school, I was always at the top of my class. I felt I had a natural knack for everything, from solving complex math problems to writing thoughtful essays on Shakespearean tragedies. I basked in the glow of praise from my teachers, admiration from my classmates and my own sense of pride in effortlessly mastering every subject that came my way. Then, I stepped into college. My freshman year was basically an extension of my earlier academic experience. I enrolled in classes that had familiar subject matter and I continued to ace them. I reveled in the ease with which I seemed to glide through college, convincing myself that my journey there would be as simple as my earlier school experiences.

Then, sophomore year rolled in and suddenly, the winds of academia shifted. The curriculum became denser, the courses more complex. For the first time, I found myself grappling with challenging concepts and I faced a bitter truth: I didn't know how to study. I had never needed any strategies before. School had always been a cakewalk. As the struggle intensified, I began to procrastinate. I delayed studying until the eleventh hour, only to find myself struggling to absorb vast quantities of information. The once familiar

A's on my report card morphed into D's and F's. I was failing my classes. I was on the brink of dropping out, my dreams teetering on the edge. My once certain trajectory now seemed murky and uncertain. My life story could have had a very different turn, had I succumbed to this struggle. Luckily, I embraced the challenge and armed myself with effective learning strategies. On the verge of academic failure, I discovered and harnessed powerful learning tools that not only helped me conquer my college years but also significantly influenced the course of my life.

Learning is a foundational skill, one that has the remarkable characteristic of building upon itself. The more adept you become at learning, the more rapidly you can assimilate new knowledge and skills, particularly those that contribute to income growth. You'll be able to understand the fundamentals of finance and investing more comprehensively, which is vital for effectively managing and growing your wealth. But the benefits extend far beyond finance. Mastering effective learning strategies will enable you to acquire additional skills, making you a more valuable asset in your workplace or business. It can help you excel in areas like leadership, project management, negotiation and strategic thinking, which are instrumental in climbing the career ladder or running a successful business.

Proficiency in learning equips you with a lifelong tool that aids in any situation in which you need to understand new concepts or acquire new skills. Whether it's adapting to new technologies, understanding evolving market trends or even learning a new language, your ability to learn effectively can expediently facilitate these processes. This core skill not only empowers you to absorb the principles and strategies discussed in this book but also prepares you for a lifetime of successful learning. This, in turn, opens up an array of opportunities for personal and professional growth, significantly enhancing your journey toward financial independence and early retirement.

Let's first explore the basic mechanisms of your brain that facilitate learning. This understanding begins with an exploration of the fundamental structure of the brain and how various regions contribute to the process of learning. Knowing how your brain processes and retains information, you can adopt strategies that align with its natural operations, thereby enhancing your learning efficiency. An integral part of this understanding is the introduction to the two primary modes of thinking: the Focused and Diffuse modes. Focused thinking refers to the concentrated, direct approach to problem solving in which your brain zeroes in on specific details. On the other hand, diffuse thinking is more about the relaxed, broad approach that allows the brain to make novel connections between disparate pieces of information. Balancing these two modes is key to effective learning. For instance, you might spend focused time studying an investment book, then take breaks allowing your mind to relax and process the information diffusely. Alternating between these modes helps prevent cognitive fatigue and promotes better understanding.

Memory plays a crucial role in your financial learning journey. The process of forming, retaining and recalling financial information and strategies is vital for practical application. Employing memory-enhancing techniques can significantly boost your learning efficiency. Spaced repetition, which involves revisiting information at increasingly extended intervals, can strengthen your recall of financial facts and strategies. The power of practice and repetition cannot be overstated. Financial acumen is rarely a byproduct of one-time study or experience. Instead, it is through continual practice and repetition that financial strategies and concepts become second nature. As you regularly engage with these concepts, you'll find yourself becoming more comfortable and proficient in making sound financial decisions, which can accelerate your path toward financial independence and early retirement.

Chunking, the practice of breaking down information into manageable portions, can be particularly useful in understanding and remembering complex concepts. For example, instead of trying to understand the entirety of how to invest, you might break it down into smaller chunks like types of assets, risk tolerance, investment strategies and so on. By digesting financial knowledge in bite-size pieces and understanding each component deeply, you'll build a robust financial understanding.

An all-too-common obstacle to efficient learning is procrastination. To combat procrastination, various time-management and productivity techniques can help. Among these, the Pomodoro Technique has proven effective for many. This method involves breaking your work into manageable, time-bound intervals, typically 25 minutes long, separated by short breaks. Implementing such techniques can help you stay focused, maintain momentum and reduce the tendency to delay essential learning tasks, all of which are crucial for mastering financial strategies and concepts.

Often overlooked in the learning process is the illusion of competence: the deceptive belief that we've understood a concept when, in fact, our grasp is superficial. This illusion can lead to overconfidence and eventually hinder progress. Approaches like active recall, in which you test your knowledge rather than simply rereading the material, or explaining the concepts to someone else, can be powerful ways to deepen comprehension and ensure mastery.

Sleep is an active period during which a lot of important processing, restoration and strengthening occurs. Specifically, it plays an indispensable role in learning and memory consolidation, processes that are crucial to expanding our knowledge base and skillset. A good night's sleep helps cement the new information we've gathered during the day, transferring it from short-term memory into long-term memory, thereby fortifying our grasp of new concepts, strategies and skills. Conversely, sleep deprivation can significantly impair our cognitive functions. Lack of sleep can lead to difficulties in concentrating, slowed thinking and reduced capacity to absorb and retain new information. Following are some practical and scientifically backed strategies that will enhance your sleep quality and optimize your sleeping routine.

1. Maintain a consistent sleep–wake cycle, even on weekends, to regulate your internal body clock.

2. Establish a presleep routine to signal your body that it's time to wind down.

3. Create a sleep-friendly environment that's dark, quiet and cool.

4. Understand the potential hindrances to good sleep, such as the blue light emitted by electronic devices.

All these tips are geared toward helping you get the restful sleep your brain needs to process and retain the wealth of information necessary for financial success. Moreover, it's vital to recognize the intrinsic link between physical health and financial well-being.

Physical exercise is more than just a method of staying fit; it's an influential catalyst for our cognitive processes. Scientific research has established a compelling correlation between regular exercise and mental acuity. It not only boosts our physical health but also facilitates the production of brain-derived neurotrophic factor (BDNF), a protein that encourages the growth and survival of neurons, thereby enhancing brain health. This improvement in brain health translates into better memory, heightened cognitive abilities and improved mood, all of which contribute to effective learning.

Exercise enhances neuroplasticity (the brain's ability to form and reorganize synaptic connections), supports memory consolidation and fosters a positive state of mind by releasing endorphins, often dubbed the body's "feel-good" hormones. But how do we reap the cognitive benefits of exercise? Activities like brisk walking during lunch breaks, a quick home workout before dinner, yoga or meditation for stress relief or even simple desk exercises for those long hours of computer usage can all be beneficial. Even minimal levels of exercise can have profound effects on cognitive function and learning.

What we eat doesn't just affect our physical health; it also plays a pivotal role in our cognitive processes, including learning. The brain, being one of the most energy-demanding organs in the body, relies heavily on the nutrients we consume. A diet rich in essential nutrients can significantly enhance brain function, memory and concentration, propelling the learning process. In contrast, a nutrient-deficient diet may lead to cognitive sluggishness, impairing our ability to grasp and retain new information effectively. Neuro-nutrition, a rapidly evolving field of research, has made significant strides in highlighting the impact of various nutrients on cognitive health. For instance, omega-3 fatty acids, found in fatty fish and flaxseeds, are crucial for brain health, while antioxidants in berries help combat oxidative stress, which can harm brain cells. On the other hand, excessive sugar intake can impair memory and cognitive flexibility. An actionable guideline for adopting a brain-healthy diet that can enhance your learning capabilities and decision-making prowess include maintaining optimal hydration levels, limiting the intake of processed foods and embracing a balanced diet rich in fruits, vegetables, lean proteins and whole grains.

In an ever-evolving world, learning cannot be confined to a particular stage of life or a specific duration. Lifelong learning is not only a tool for personal and professional development; it's a mindset that involves continuous curiosity, openness to new experiences and the pursuit of knowledge throughout life.

Upskilling Through Education and Training

More often than not, advanced education serves as the most reliable conduit to an elevated income. My grandfather, a hardworking and honorable man, nonetheless spent his life laboring strenuously, only to scrape by. It was a challenging existence, one that left little room for upward mobility. Having been granted the opportunity to access education, my father broke the cycle. He was able to acquire the knowledge, skills and credentials that enabled him to step beyond the confines of his inherited socioeconomic status. The doors of opportunity that were closed to my grandfather swung open for my father, all thanks to education.

It's not difficult to imagine that my own story might have mirrored theirs had the transformative power of education not continued its influence. If my father had not had access to education, I too would likely have been born into the same circumstances, facing the same socioeconomic limitations that my grandfather experienced. Education, thus, has not only shaped my father's life but has also played a significant role in defining my own path, setting me on a trajectory vastly different from what might have been.

Education, manifesting in various forms, occupies an influential position in today's economic landscape. Whether it's a conventional university degree, a technical or vocational program or even a thorough online certification, education arms us with the necessary instruments to traverse our professional terrains. But why does education wield such paramount importance in the current economy and how does it dovetail with our quest to maximize income? Let's dissect this further.

The primary and arguably most apparent value of education lies in the proficiency and knowledge it bestows. Irrespective of the discipline, education offers a methodical mode of learning. It forms the foundational base for understanding a subject or field, imparting us with theories, principles and practical applications that constitute the basis of our professions.

However, the merit of education extends beyond mere knowledge acquisition; it also plays a crucial role in credentialing. A degree or certification broadcasts to prospective employers that you've attained a specific level of expertise in your domain. In many professions, particularly those in highly competitive sectors, possessing a relevant educational credential is a prerequisite to even be regarded for a role. The worth of this credential escalates as you ascend the career ladder, frequently becoming the distinguishing factor when promotions and salary increments are considered.

Another noteworthy value of education, particularly higher education, resides in the networks it cultivates. Colleges or technical schools assemble cohorts of like-minded individuals, nurturing connections that often persist into professional careers. These networks can offer support, mentorship and opportunities, unlocking doors that might otherwise stay sealed. The age-old adage, "It's not just what you know, but who you know," rings true in this context.

Education nurtures critical thinking, problem-solving acumen and creativity, competencies that are highly prized in the dynamic economic landscape of today. As automation and artificial intelligence revolutionize the job market, these uniquely human skills are gaining more prominence. Employers are on the hunt for individuals who can think on their feet, adjust to change and contribute innovative ideas, all skills sharpened by quality education.

Let's discuss the concrete figures. Multiple studies have established a robust correlation between education attainment and income. Data from the U.S. Bureau of Labor Statistics indicate that bachelor's degree holders earn a median weekly income that's 67% higher than those with only a high school diploma. For those with professional degrees, the median weekly income nearly triples. While these figures represent averages and there are certainly outliers, the trend is clear: higher education often equates to higher income. The value of education in today's economy is multi-dimensional. It encapsulates skills and knowledge, credentials and networks, critical thinking and creativity. It's also intrinsically linked to the potential for a higher income.

From a statistical standpoint, advanced education remains one of the most impactful mechanisms to boost your income. Per a report from the Georgetown University Center on Education and the Workforce, those with a bachelor's degree amass, on average, about $1 million more in lifetime earnings compared to those with merely a high school diploma. Isn't that a remarkable figure? And that's just the mean value; in some fields, the income disparity can be substantially larger.

If you're currently weighing your options for a major or field of study, consider the tangible returns on your educational investment. While it's widely acknowledged that STEM disciplines (science, technology, engineering and mathematics) often lead to high-paying careers, the nuances of transitioning skills into these fields might not be as obvious. For instance, if you have a passion for writing and aim to maximize income, you might explore avenues like technical writing, editing medical texts or drafting software documentation. Alternatively, if you have a flair for design, the worlds of user experience (UX) or user interface (UI) design for tech products could be appealing. And for those who excel in communication and presentation, roles in tech sales or project management might be an ideal fit. By recognizing and aligning your inherent talents with STEM opportunities, you can carve out a path that's both fulfilling and financially advantageous.

Central to the growing significance of STEM degrees is the ongoing digital revolution. As technology relentlessly advances at an unprecedented pace, the demand for individuals who can comprehend, innovate and utilize technology grows in tandem. From artificial intelligence and data science to biotechnology and environmental engineering, STEM graduates are spearheading solutions to some of the world's most urgent challenges and enticing opportunities. STEM careers rank among the most rapidly growing and high earning jobs in the contemporary job market. As per the U.S. Bureau of Labor Statistics, STEM occupation employment expanded by 10.5% from 2009 to 2015, contrasting with a 5.2% growth in non-STEM occupations. Not only that, STEM jobs are expected to grow twice as fast as non-STEM jobs through 2031. The median annual wage for STEM jobs was considerably higher, nearly double the median wage for all other jobs. According to a New York Federal Reserve study in 2023, here are the top ten majors by median salary within five years of graduation for U.S. full-time workers with a bachelor's degree:

1. Chemical engineering, $75,000
2. Computer engineering, $74,000
3. Computer science, $73,000
4. Aerospace engineering, $72,000
5. Electrical engineering, $70,000
6. Industrial engineering, $70,000
7. Mechanical engineering, $70,000

8. Miscellaneous engineering, $68,000

9. Business analytics, $66,000

10. Civil engineering, $65,000

Engineering majors also make the most money later in their careers. Here's what the top ten median salaries look like for those who are 35 to 45 years old.

1. Chemical engineering, $120,000

2. Computer engineering, $114,000

3. Aerospace engineering, $112,000

4. Electrical engineering, $109,000

5. Computer science, $105,000

6. Mechanical engineering, $105,000

7. Miscellaneous physical sciences, $104,000

8. Industrial engineering, $100,000

9. Miscellaneous engineering, $100,000

10. Civil engineering, $100,000

In addition, a STEM degree often arms graduates with a spectrum of transferable skills. These include analytical acumen, problem solving, creativity and adaptability, all of which are coveted in today's dynamic job market. Regardless of the specific domain they eventually land in, STEM graduates are often well equipped to excel and progress. With technology increasingly permeating every facet of our lives and industries, the demand for STEM skills is poised to continue growing. Even non-STEM jobs increasingly demand a degree of digital proficiency. As a consequence, individuals with a STEM education are likely to have a competitive edge in the future job market.

And don't forget, your education shouldn't halt once you step out of the classroom. The individuals who achieve the greatest success are those who endorse lifelong learning. Stay abreast of industry trends. Pursue additional courses if necessary. Your degree or certification can get your foot in the door, but your dedication to learning and evolving will assist you in ascending the career ladder.

Concentrating on Your Strengths: The Power of Focus

The idea of a side hustle is an almost irresistible attraction to some people. The very term conjures a certain appeal, a spirit of resistance, a hint of entrepreneurial flare. A person with a side hustle projects an image of an achiever, someone who isn't complacent with the norm, someone ready to toil after hours in the quest to fulfill their aspirations. This narrative has been promoted through numerous articles, blogs, podcasts and social media posts: "Kick-start a side hustle, earn supplemental income and seize command of your financial future." But does the actuality of the side hustle measure up to its glamorous depiction?

First and foremost, it's vital to recognize that a side hustle, inherently, is an occupation pursued outside of your primary job. It demands time, effort and often, a substantial mental shift from your regular work. It goes beyond merely squeezing a few extra hours into your week; it's about managing multiple responsibilities, meeting diverse expectations and alternating between distinct modes of thinking and working.

This balancing act can give rise to numerous complications. Side hustles can encroach on your leisure time, extending your work hours and potentially impacting your health and well-being. They can also split your focus, implying that neither your primary job nor your side hustle receive the full advantage of your skills. There's also the risk of conflict. What if your side hustle competes with your main job, interferes with your work obligations or even breaches your employment contract?

Moreover, there's the issue of financial gain. Indeed, a side hustle can generate an additional income source, but is it dependable and enduring? After considering the time and resources expended, is the net profit substantial? And could that time and energy have been more effectively utilized in your main job, where the prospects for financial return might be higher and steadier? While side hustles can present benefits and opportunities, they also carry potential drawbacks that are often disregarded in the popular discourse. As with everything in life, it's about making enlightened choices, and when it comes to the allure of the side hustle, it's beneficial to scrutinize the realities.

The notion of maintaining one or two side gigs in addition to your primary job might seem like a perfect way to earn some additional income. And certainly, it can be successful for some. However, from my experience, attempting to balance multiple jobs often results in divided focus, reduced productivity and eventually, a potential decline in the quality of your work in each role. Here's the catch: when you're stretched thin across multiple gigs, you're likely to struggle in delivering the level of commitment, time and energy that each job warrants. This leads to a stagnation in your skills development and overall career progression, both of which are crucial factors in augmenting your income over time. Instead of dispersing yourself across several jobs, why not direct your energy into one role that truly sparks your passion?

What would happen if you channeled all your time and energy into becoming an outstanding software engineer? Instead of just clocking in and out of your regular job, you could be constantly learning new programming languages, staying up to date with industry trends and networking with other professionals in your field. You would be rendering yourself invaluable to your employer and when it's time for promotions or project assignments, you're the first choice.

A wealth of evidence suggests that the path to expertise involves concentrated focus and intentional practice. When you reach a high level of skill in a specific area, you're more likely to command higher pay. In a time when multitasking is often applauded, we tend to overlook the fact that our brains are not designed to handle multiple tasks efficiently. When we fragment our attention, we essentially water down our focus, making it challenging to dive deep and perform optimally. However, when we concentrate on a single task or job, we can go deeper, learn more, perform better and, ultimately, boost our earning potential. When you devote your time, energy and mental resources to one job, you're not just working; you're mastering. You're comprehending the intricacies of your role, understanding the dynamics of your industry and becoming an expert in your field. And this level of expertise often leads to career progression, better job prospects and increased income.

Consider the realm of sports. Athletes like Serena Williams or Lionel Messi didn't reach the zenith of their careers by trying their hand at several sports. They chose one sport and trained relentlessly, focusing all their energy and attention on honing their skills. The result? Unmatched success and substantial financial rewards.

Similarly, in the corporate world, individuals who concentrate on a single job or field tend to progress faster than those who scatter themselves across multiple roles or sectors. They're able to develop a deep understanding of their work, exhibit superior performance and earn the acknowledgment and rewards associated with being a top performer. By focusing on one job, you also have the time and energy to invest in ongoing learning and skill development, which can further augment your value and earning potential. You can establish robust professional networks, seek mentorships and take on ambitious projects, all of which can pave the way to new opportunities and higher income.

Naturally, this doesn't mean that you shouldn't venture into other interests or opportunities. However, when the goal is to enhance your income, the effectiveness of focus cannot be ignored. It's about choosing depth over breadth, excellence over average performance.

Some individuals assume that undertaking more tasks, managing more responsibilities and working extended hours will inevitably yield better results and a higher income. However, the truth may be quite different. There is an increasing amount of evidence suggesting that concentrating on fewer tasks and executing them well can lead to enhanced productivity, improved performance and ultimately, increased income. This is the doctrine of "efficiency over quantity," or as I prefer to label it, "the power of doing less to achieve more." First, let's debunk the myth that longer working hours equate to increased productivity. Numerous studies indicate that productivity tends to decrease after a certain number of hours worked in a week, with one study suggesting that productivity begins to diminish after 50 hours and drops significantly after 55 hours. Essentially, you might be dedicating more time but achieving less.

Moreover, excessive working hours can lead to burnout, a state of physical and mental fatigue that can drastically affect your work performance and overall health. Burnout can result in decreased productivity, increased errors and can even impact your personal relationships and health. From an income maximization perspective, the risk of burnout simply isn't worth it.

Let's consider the power of focusing on fewer tasks. When you're not scattering your attention across various tasks or jobs, you can provide your full attention to each task at hand. This allows you to work more efficiently, deliver higher quality work and accomplish more in less time. It also encourages deeper learning and skill development, which can elevate your value in the workplace and enhance your income potential.

Narrowing your focus to fewer tasks can also improve work–life balance, which has been shown to increase job satisfaction, reduce stress and foster better health—all factors that can indirectly contribute to income maximization by enhancing job performance and reducing sick days. Of course, every rule has its exceptions and every situation has its unique aspects. But based on my experience, concentrating your energy on mastering one thing often proves to be more profitable in the long run. It's about working intelligently, not exhaustively; it's about prioritizing quality over quantity; it's about utilizing the power of focus to maximize efficiency and income.

Choosing the Right Workplace

It might seem obvious, but it merits emphasis: the location of your work and the organization you work for can notably influence your income. It's common knowledge that job roles in major cities often attract higher salaries than those in smaller towns or rural regions.

Similarly, larger, renowned companies tend to offer more attractive compensation packages than their smaller counterparts.

Here's a tangible example: data from the U.S. Bureau of Labor Statistics shows that the average annual salary in the New York Metropolitan area was $74,870 in 2022. Contrastingly, the same statistic for the nonmetropolitan region of Central Kentucky was $51,490. That's a considerable variance in earning potential based solely on location. Beyond the charm of glittering city lights and urban thrill, cities, particularly the large ones, serve as economic powerhouses that provide significant opportunities for income maximization. Cities are typically home to a vast spectrum of industries and organizations, including several top-tier companies and startups. This diversity presents a plethora of job opportunities, as well as the flexibility to switch industries or roles without needing to change your residence. Whether your field is technology, finance, health care, creative arts or any other sector, you're likely to discover numerous job choices in a major city.

Competition in cities tends to be intense, among businesses as well as job applicants. This competitive environment can elevate salaries, as companies strive to attract and retain the top talent. Consequently, jobs in major cities often offer higher compensation than similar roles in smaller towns or rural areas. Consider tech behemoths like Google and Meta (formerly Facebook). In 2022, the median compensation at Google was $279,902, while at Meta, it was $296,320. Contrastingly, the median household income in the United States in 2022 was $70,784, according to the U.S.

Census Bureau. This comparison illustrates the generous pay scales of these top tech companies.

Cities also provide ample opportunities for networking and professional growth. From industry conferences and meetups to business seminars and training programs, there's always an event that can help you widen your professional network, enhance your skill set and advance your career prospects. It's a self-perpetuating cycle. The best cities host the best jobs, which attract the best talent, leading to even better businesses and funding concentrating in these cities. This phenomenon is known as the "agglomeration economy"—a concentration of firms and people that, in turn, draws more individuals and companies, thus perpetuating a cycle that continues to increase wages.

One notable shift we've witnessed in recent years is the emergence of remote work. Embedded within this trend lies an advantageous arbitrage opportunity: the prospect of earning a big city income while residing in a low-cost area. It works like this: Several progressive companies, many of which are leading players in their respective fields, have implemented location-agnostic pay policies. These companies base their salaries on job roles and market rates, rather than the employee's location. Therefore, you could be operating from a small town or a lower cost city, yet earning a salary comparable to what you'd earn if you resided in San Francisco or New York. This setup offers an optimal combination. You enjoy the financial advantage of a high salary, paired with the lower living expenses typical of smaller cities or towns. The potential savings can be significant, particularly when you consider the high housing costs in many large cities. You'd possess the same earning capacity, but your dollars would stretch much further in terms of housing, groceries and other living expenses.

Why should you aim to work at a top-tier company? When it comes to amplifying your income, aiming for the top can often prove beneficial, both in the immediate future and over the course of your career. Primarily, top-tier companies often offer top-tier salaries. These are organizations that are pioneering in their respective industries. They're typically highly profitable, growing and eager to attract and retain superior talent. One of the strategies they employ to achieve this is providing competitive salaries and benefits packages.

Besides higher salaries, top-tier companies frequently provide comprehensive benefits packages. These can comprise health insurance, retirement contributions, paid leave and other perks that enhance your overall financial stability. Some companies present stock options or profit sharing schemes, granting employees a stake in the company's prosperity. Being employed by a leading company can considerably elevate your career path. These companies are typically at the forefront of their industries, implying that you'll gain exposure to the newest technologies, concepts and industry trends. You'll also find opportunities for professional growth and promotion, which can incrementally raise your earning potential.

Having a prestigious company listed on your resume can unlock future opportunities. It's a clear signal to prospective employers that you've been scrutinized and approved by an industry leader and that you have the capability to perform exceptionally. This can make you a more desirable candidate for future job openings, providing you with the leverage to negotiate higher pay. Also, by working with extremely talented individuals (because top companies can afford to be quite selective in their hiring process), you benefit greatly. For example, Google's acceptance rate for full-time positions is even lower than institutions like Harvard. Owing to their reputation, resources and selective hiring practices, top companies often attract the industry's cream of the crop.

The benefits of working with such a talented cohort are numerous. First, it's incredibly inspiring. Being surrounded by high achievers can propel you to perform your best, push your boundaries and aspire to excellence. It can instill in you a sense of ambition and determination that may be lacking in a less competitive environment. Second, you can learn a tremendous amount from your colleagues. They can introduce you to new ideas, skills and viewpoints that you may not otherwise come across. This kind of learning environment can foster personal growth and development, which, in turn, can enhance your career and income potential. Third, the connections and relationships you forge at a top company can benefit your long-term career. Your colleagues could transform into future business partners, mentors or even employers. They could offer references, job leads and other forms of support as you progress in your career.

A question I frequently encounter from job seekers is, "Will I have to work more hours at these top-tier companies?" The response is, "Not necessarily." There's a widespread presumption that a higher paying job at a prestigious company will consume more of your time, thereby disrupting the work–life balance. However, in my experience, the reality is far more complex.

First, let's dispel a common myth: Higher compensation doesn't necessarily equate to longer hours or less balance. Your work–life balance tends to be more significantly influenced by your immediate manager and the specifics of your job role than any overarching company culture. While the company's ethos plays a role, your direct supervisor and your daily tasks bear much more significance. Throughout my professional journey, I've experienced the dynamics of various organizations, emerging startups, mid-scale firms and renowned tech behemoths. A vital insight I've gathered is that there isn't a linear relationship between the compensation you receive and the work–life balance you achieve. I've encountered roles that are highly remunerative yet demand reasonable working hours, as well as less lucrative positions that require a disproportionate amount of time and effort.

Now, let's address another prevalent assumption, the notion that ascending the corporate hierarchy inevitably leads to an increased workload. While career advancement often comes with added responsibilities, it doesn't necessarily equate to more "work" in the conventional sense. Consider the evolution of a software engineer's career for instance. As you transition from being an individual contributor to taking on a leadership role, the nature of your tasks undergoes a significant shift. The hours spent absorbed in lines of code, typing away on your keyboard, start to decrease. Instead, your schedule becomes increasingly filled with meetings, strategic deliberations, team management duties and decision-making obligations. Your professional role morphs, you're no longer just a programmer; you become a visionary, a strategist, a mentor. This transformation demands a heightened level of experience, a more diverse skill set and a more comprehensive understanding of the business. It indeed involves a different kind of "work," one that leans heavily toward intellectual and emotional exertion, rather than physical labor.

To summarize, the wisdom gleaned from these experiences and data is clear: Strive to work for the most esteemed company you can, located in the most appealing city to you.

Getting an Interview

The job search process often begins with a single document: your résumé. This seemingly simple piece of paper can determine whether you secure an interview or get passed over. Think of your résumé as your professional highlight reel. It's your chance to showcase your skills, experience and accomplishments succinctly. However, recruiters typically spend just ten seconds scanning a résumé; you need to make an immediate impact. Many résumés these days are screened by automated processes before they even reach a recruiter's desk. That's why it's essential to create a document that is not only visually appealing but also contains the right content. Crafting a compelling résumé involves more than just outlining your skills, experiences and qualifications. The language and presentation you choose can make all the difference. Here's a quick primer to ensure you're using the most effective language and avoiding common pitfalls.

Begin your bullet points with action verbs to give your résumé a dynamic and assertive tone. When writing your résumé, strive for specificity over generality. Use active language and express your achievements honestly, avoiding overly complex or "flowery" descriptions. Aim for fact-based statements and quantify your accomplishments where possible. Keep in mind, your résumé is written for people who scan quickly, so make every word count.

Here's a checklist to help you avoid the most common mistakes people make on their résumés:

- Steer clear of personal pronouns like "I."
- Abstain from using abbreviations that might not be universally understood.
- Skip the narrative style and opt for concise bullet points.
- Avoid using slang or colloquial expressions.
- Refrain from including a picture unless specifically asked.
- Omit personal details such as age or gender.

- Do not include references; provide them only when asked.
- Don't lead each line with a date; it disrupts the readability of your résumé.
- Eliminate spelling and grammar errors: Proofread your résumé multiple times and have a friend or mentor review it.
- Include contact information: Make sure your email address and phone number are included and correct.
- Customize your résumé to align with the specific requirements of the job you're applying for.

A great résumé is concise and to the point. Limit your résumé to one page, particularly if you have fewer than ten years of experience. Formatting is crucial to ensuring readability, so use a professional font, bullet points for easy scanning and bold headings create sections.

If your GPA isn't particularly impressive, feel free to omit it. However, if you've scored a GPA of 3.5 or higher, it can highlight your academic accomplishments. Keep in mind that after your first job, recruiters typically value skills and experience more than educational credentials.

Finally, here are a few more things to keep in mind as you write your résumé:
- Maintain uniformity in format and content.
- Strike a balance between text and white space to enhance readability.

- Employ consistent spacing, bold text and capitalization for emphasis.

- Prioritize sections, such as "Experience," according to their relevance.

- Present information within each section in reverse chronological order.

- Steer clear of unexplained career timeline gaps.

- Verify that your formatting is preserved when converted to a PDF or other formats.

What about cover letters? Your cover letter is effectively a writing sample and preview of your communication skills. Here are some guidelines for effective cover letters:

- **Personalize your letter:** Address the letter to the appropriate contact person whenever possible. If the job ad doesn't specify a name, a bit of research might uncover who will be reviewing applications.

- **Do your homework:** Research about the organization, its culture and the role you're applying for will help you tailor your cover letter effectively.

- **Be concise and clear:** Keep your cover letter short, usually no more than a page, and focus on being clear and factual. Avoid unnecessary verbosity.

- **Provide concrete examples:** Bolster your claims about your skills and qualifications with concrete examples that demonstrate your competency.

- **Consider the employer's perspective:** Put yourself in the employer's shoes to contemplate what kind of assurance would convince them that you can handle the job effectively.

- **Minimize "I" usage:** While your cover letter should focus on your qualifications, try not to overuse "I." It can make your letter seem self-centered.

- **Use action words:** A marketing tool in essence, your cover letter should be packed with action verbs that bring your experiences and skills to life.

- **Refer to the job description:** Make explicit connections between your abilities and the requirements listed in the job description.

- **Maintain consistency in formatting:** Ensure that your cover letter and résumé share the same font type and size for a cohesive look.

Those starting out in their careers often find themselves caught in the seemingly inescapable catch-22 of job hunting: The necessity of experience to land a job, but the challenge of gaining that experience without having had a job in the first place. Fortunately, internships present a viable solution to this paradox.

Internships are purpose-built opportunities for students, granting them the chance to gather relevant experience before they venture into the professional sphere. These temporary roles not only enable one to earn some money but also plunge you into the midst of a chosen industry, offering a direct experience of authentic job situations. Incorporating an internship, or even better, several internships, into your résumé can considerably strengthen your profile. This extra layer of experience can differentiate you from the throng of fresh graduates seeking the same positions. It communicates to prospective employers that you've already familiarized yourself with a professional setting and are earnestly committed to your career path. In reality, employers invariably prefer candidates with practical, hands-on experience in the relevant field. Endeavor to secure at least two internships during your college years.

So, how does one unearth these golden opportunities? Career fairs hosted by your university serve as an excellent springboard, as numerous companies are actively on the lookout for talent from certain academic institutions. Additionally, online job platforms provide a plethora of internship opportunities both nationally and even globally. Don't allow geographic constraints to deter you; many companies are prepared to cover your travel expenses and sometimes offer housing allowances for internships located out of state. Bear in mind, internships are primarily designed to benefit you, the intern. Although they provide practical experience, they recognize that your main objective is to learn. Therefore, the pressure to perform is typically less intense, creating a conducive environment for you to evolve, acquire new skills and prepare for your future professional path.

Securing an internship can sometimes seem intimidating. The competition can be stiff and not all candidates manage to land these sought-after positions. However, the absence of an internship or job experience doesn't equate to a dead-end. You can compensate by engaging in personal projects. Undertaking personal projects is an excellent alternative that can showcase your skills, enthusiasm and proactive approach to potential employers. While these projects may not replace professional experience, they are extremely valuable, often demonstrating your capacity to work independently and your eagerness to explore and learn beyond formal settings.

The key is to choose a project that genuinely captivates you, rather than something commonplace or "anticipated." When you're passionate about your work, you tend to learn more and the results are usually more notable. Additionally, discussing your project with zeal and knowledge in an interview context makes for an engaging conversation. The most profitable hobby project I ever embarked on brought in more income than a summer internship. I ventured into the world of video games, focusing on a popular game called Diablo III, which included an in-game auction house where players could trade items for real money. I developed a trading bot that bought and sold items based on specific criteria quicker than any human could. Although my account was eventually suspended after a couple of weeks and the game's auction house was ultimately shut down, the project was enjoyable and made a substantial amount of money for a college student. So, if internships are out of your reach, engaging in personal projects that fascinate you is an excellent alternative.

But what if you're already a working professional? In that case, referrals are your strongest option. A referral occurs when someone familiar with your work recommends you for a position in their organization or elsewhere. This could be a current or former coworker, a friend or even an acquaintance knowledgeable about your abilities and experience. The effectiveness of referrals in the job search process is frequently underrated. They can lead to opportunities that may not even be publicly advertised. Why is that? Companies have faith in their employees' judgment. If an employee is willing to put their reputation on the line by recommending someone for a job, that candidate is likely to be taken into serious consideration. In fact, many companies run employee referral programs to motivate their staff to recommend potential candidates. These programs can be incredibly successful. A LinkedIn report suggests that while only about 7% of job applicants are referrals, they account for approximately 40% of all hires.

Utilizing your professional connections for job referrals can give you a competitive advantage. These connections can often provide insightful details about the company's work environment, expectations for the role and recruitment procedure, which can increase your chances of success. In addition, candidates who come in through referrals often experience quicker hiring processes and exhibit higher retention rates compared to those discovered through other means.

So, how do you secure a referral? The simplest approach is to reach out to your existing professional network, including former coworkers, bosses and even clients or customers. Inform them about your interest in exploring new job opportunities. Be specific about the roles that interest you and why you think you are a good fit for them. And remember, networking involves give and take. Be ready to offer your support in return and be open to reciprocating in a similar situation.

If you don't have any referrals, don't worry. You can directly contact hiring managers and recruiters on LinkedIn. LinkedIn, the world's biggest professional networking platform, is often underutilized in job hunting. It allows you to showcase your professional persona and directly connect with hiring managers and recruiters. To leverage LinkedIn for your job search, first, make sure your LinkedIn profile is professional and up-to-date. This includes having a professional profile photo, an appealing headline, an informative summary and a thorough listing of your skills, experiences and qualifications. When your profile is polished, identify the companies of interest. Follow their company pages to stay updated about new job postings and company announcements. LinkedIn's advanced search feature also lets you identify individuals related to these companies, like hiring managers and recruiters. Send them a connection request and more importantly, personalize your message. Be respectful and brief. State your reason for reaching out and express your interest in the company and the role. Highlight how your skills and experience make you an appropriate candidate. This strategy is often more beneficial than crafting a cover letter and a more efficient use of your time. By directly reaching out to a real person, you can potentially bypass automated processes that filter out résumés.

Applying directly on a company's website remains the most common way of securing a job. It's how I've landed most of my jobs. Don't be too disheartened if you don't receive an immediate response, or any response at all. Hiring processes can greatly vary from one company to another. The more positions you apply for, the higher your chances of landing an interview. This approach requires perseverance and tenacity, but remember that each application brings you one step closer to securing your desired role.

Interviewing Effectively

There was a time when I doubted my ability to secure a position at a leading tech firm, believing I fell short of the mark. As a newly minted computer engineering graduate, I dreamed of landing a job in one of the big tech companies. But an internal voice echoed the same message over and over, "You're not good enough." These were companies that demanded the cream of the crop and in my eyes, I was anything but. Yet, a pivotal moment changed my perspective. It was when one of my classmates, who I had always considered my equal in skills and intellect, obtained a role at Google. This news stirred something in me. It was a sudden realization that if someone like him could breach the barriers to big tech, then maybe I could, too. Maybe I had been shackling myself with a self-imposed limit that was based on unfounded beliefs rather than facts. With newfound determination, I decided to change my approach. I invested myself in meticulous interview preparation. My days became filled with studying, practicing coding problems and doing mock interviews. I gave up weekends and weeknights to delve into complex algorithms and data structures. It paid off when I secured a role at a FAANG company with an annual compensation exceeding $500,000.

Securing that coveted job offer hinges on your performance during the interview. This fact can be quite daunting, but with thorough preparation and the right mindset, you can enter the process confidently and significantly boost your odds of success. There's a well-known saying, "Luck is what happens when preparation meets opportunity." When it comes to job interviews, this couldn't ring truer. The degree of your preparation is directly proportional to your likelihood of success. Let's get into the essential elements of effective interview readiness.

Understand the company

Your interview preparation should start with gaining an in-depth understanding of the company you aspire to join. Familiarize yourself with their products or services, their mission, ethos and organizational culture. Grasp the industry they operate within and any challenges they may be encountering. Research recent news articles, press releases and any available public information about the company. This wealth of knowledge will not only enable you to tailor your responses in the interview but also demonstrate to the interviewer that your interest in the company is genuine. Companies that place emphasis on culture want to ensure that you're a fit. The right skills are the baseline; they also need someone who will mesh well with their existing team. Devote time to understanding the company's culture and values, reflecting on how your own values align. Demonstrating this cultural alignment throughout your interview is crucial.

Understand the role

Make a concerted effort to scrutinize the job description for the role you're vying for. Comprehend the required skills, qualifications and responsibilities. Visualize yourself in that position and consider how your past experience aligns with it. This mental exercise will equip you to express convincingly why you're the ideal candidate for the role during the interview. Your goal is to demonstrate that not only are you qualified for the job but that you're superior to all other contenders. Nailing the technical questions is usually a given. If the job is desirable, it will attract a lot of competition. Many of the applicants will be qualified. Passing the technical round and proceeding to behavioral questions is only possible if you've answered all the technical questions correctly. For software engineers, this typically involves months of preparation. Using resources such as LeetCode (a website providing hundreds of algorithms and data structure problems), reviewing the Technical Interview Handbook (a GitHub repository offering extensive information on technical interviews) and refreshing your knowledge using the System Design Primer (a guide on how to design large-scale systems) are tried-and-true methods. I, along with thousands of other engineers, have successfully leveraged these resources to secure roles at prestigious companies like Meta, Amazon, Apple, Netflix and Google. Your profession may have other technical requirements, so it's important to familiarize yourself with the professional standards of your industry.

Predict interview questions

Each interview is unique, but there are common questions that tend to arise frequently. Questions about your strengths and weaknesses, your interest in the role or your handling of previous challenges are pretty standard. Make sure to allocate some time to consider these questions and develop concise, well-considered responses. Bear in mind that your delivery is just as important as your content. Attempting to conjure up answers spontaneously can result in unstructured and incoherent responses, a situation you should strive to avoid.

Conduct mock interviews

Practicing your answers with a friend is very beneficial. Strive to simulate the actual interview environment as closely as possible. Dress as you would for the real interview, situate yourself in a quiet, professional setting and communicate as you would in the actual interview. This practice will ease your ability to articulate your thoughts and decrease the chances of faltering during the real interview. Practice is often underestimated when it comes to job interviews, yet its importance cannot be overstated. Familiarizing yourself with your responses boosts your confidence, enabling clear and convincing expression of your thoughts. It lessens uncertainty and stress, allowing you to present the best version of yourself. Job interviews can be likened to performances; the best actors don't ad lib on stage. They rehearse until their roles are second nature.

Now that you're equipped with some fundamental principles for job interview preparation, let's explore the most effective strategy for responding to non-technical behavioral questions: the STAR method. Behavioral interview questions generally prompt candidates to share examples from their past experience that exhibit specific skills or behaviors. These can encompass teamwork and problem solving, leadership and conflict resolution, among others.

The STAR method is a highly effective approach for structuring responses to such questions.

STAR, an acronym for Situation, Task, Action and Result, is a powerful tool for structuring your responses. Here's an in-depth explanation:

Situation: Begin by outlining the scenario. Paint a picture of the specific context or backdrop you were operating within. Be precise, but brief. An example might be, "During my tenure as a project manager at XYZ Corp, we were given the mandate to launch a new product within a strict three-month deadline."

Task: Explain your individual role in that scenario. What were you accountable for? What hurdle or issue did you confront? For instance, you could say, "I was tasked with the leadership of a six-person team to conceptualize, validate and promote the new product."

Action: Then, describe the particular actions you undertook to tackle the task. Highlight your own contributions rather than the collective effort of your team or your superior's input. This is your opportunity to illustrate how you tackle obstacles and devise solutions. For example, you could mention, "I formulated a comprehensive project blueprint, allocated specific duties to team members and established a weekly touch-base to track progress and adapt our approach as needed."

Result: Ultimately, share the consequence of your actions. Attempt to quantify the outcome, if feasible. Did you achieve the objective? What insights did you gain from the experience?

You might say, "We managed to launch the product a fortnight ahead of the deadline, leading to a considerable surge in the company's Q4 revenue. This experience underscored for me the significance of transparent communication and proactive project management."

While leveraging the STAR method, it's vital to concentrate on actions that demonstrate your skills and talents in a manner aligned with the company's culture and values. Suppose, for example, the company values bold risk-taking and swift execution. You would want to narrate stories that reflect how you embody these values. It wouldn't be particularly relevant to share a story about your meticulous attention to detail and gradual execution, would it?

Negotiating Successfully

Kudos on securing the job offer; now it's time to ensure you get the maximum compensation possible. Mastering negotiation skills can significantly boost your overall earnings, which could cumulatively result in an additional hundreds of thousands, if not millions, over your career. Most individuals will only engage in job offer negotiations a dozen times or fewer throughout their lives, while the professionals you negotiate with do it for a living. This naturally places you at a disadvantage. I'm here to provide you with the most effective strategies for maximizing your job offer.

Negotiation should always be on the table. Many applicants hesitate to engage in salary discussions due to discomfort or fear of possible backlash. There's a common concern that discussing salary or initiating negotiations might lead to the withdrawal of the offer. However, these fears are largely baseless, and understanding why can help alleviate these concerns and empower you to negotiate with greater confidence.

It's important to grasp the significant investment a company makes during the hiring process. They've sifted through hundreds, or even thousands, of résumés; conducted multiple interview rounds; involved various team members (including busy senior staff); and likely incurred considerable costs such as recruitment fees and advertisement expenses. This process can span weeks or even months. When a company extends an offer, it signifies their selection of you among numerous candidates. They've dedicated substantial time, effort and financial resources to arrive at this stage. Therefore, it's highly improbable that they will retract the offer simply because you initiated salary negotiation. In fact, most employers anticipate a degree of negotiation during the hiring process. Negotiating your salary doesn't imply greed or suggest that you're not a team player. It demonstrates that you appreciate the value of your skills and experiences and have a clear grasp of your market worth.

So, where should you begin? First, recognize your value. Here, research is pivotal. Utilize resources like Glassdoor, Blind, Payscale, Levels.fyi and LinkedIn to find salary ranges for your role. These platforms offer a wealth of information about salaries across various industries, companies and roles. This data can help you gauge the compensation range for your role, considering factors like your experience, the industry, the size of the company and the location. Also, keep in mind that compensation isn't solely about the base salary. Elements like sign-on bonuses, stock options and benefits are equally vital and should be included in your valuation of worth. Knowledge is power and the more you know about industry salary standards, the more robust your position in the negotiation process.

Recruiters are known for probing your salary expectations. There are several strategies to navigate this situation. One method is to reflect the question back to the recruiter, inquiring about the salary bracket for the position. This maneuver often shifts the focus from your expectations to the company's budget or typical remuneration structure for the role. However, you may face a scenario in which the recruiter is hesitant to reveal the salary bracket, pressing you to offer a specific figure instead. Here, you can choose from several tactics. One is to evade by underlining your concentration on the role and the company, articulating something like, "At this point, my main concern is determining if this role aligns well with my skills and career aspirations. I'm confident that if we both agree it's a suitable match, we can arrive at a mutually satisfactory compensation package." Alternatively, if you feel compelled to provide a number, refer to the upper limit of the salary range you've identified through your research. Stating something like, "Considering my comprehension of the role and the market, I reckon a salary within the range of X to Y would be fitting," can showcase that you've done your due diligence and are cognizant of your market worth. The final option is to simply decline to respond and insist they present an offer first. If you have multiple offers, this could prompt each company to compete in a blind auction.

It's always best to negotiate from a position of strength. This principle applies equally to job offers. The party with more and better alternatives invariably holds the upper hand. One of the most powerful strategies to augment your bargaining power is to secure multiple job offers at the same time. Companies, too, are prone to FOMO (fear of missing out). Google, for instance, is notorious for extending top-of-the-range offers only to candidates who also have a competing offer from Meta. In job negotiations, your role and seniority level usually define a specific salary range. Your goal should invariably be to negotiate a salary near the top end of that band. In some cases, if you demonstrate extraordinary value or adeptly leverage multiple offers, you could even negotiate a salary beyond the typical range with special authorizations.

Another tactic recruiters and hiring managers frequently use is to solicit your opinion immediately after extending an offer. It's preferable to postpone your response, particularly if you're still undergoing other interviews. Moreover, it's generally advisable to avoid being rushed into providing an immediate response. A simple way to do this is by stating, "I'll need to discuss this with a friend/partner/parent."

When you've collected all the job offers you're anticipating, it's time to tactically leverage them against each other. The key is to be honest but considerate. Inform them that you've garnered other offers with more substantial total compensation. Your objective here isn't to create a hostile bidding war, but to underscore your market value. Craft your message in a way that centers on the predicament you're in, rather than appearing to issue an ultimatum. For example, you might express, "I'm incredibly enthusiastic about the prospect of joining your team, but I've also received an equally competitive offer from another firm. I'm drawn to the potential role here and I'm wondering if there's anything we can do to make this offer more compelling." They'll likely inquire about which company made the offer and the exact amount involved. Most recruiters and hiring managers have a solid grasp of the compensation landscape, so it's unwise to fabricate details. Whether or not you reveal the names of the other companies is entirely your call, but bear in mind that well-established and prestigious companies can lend significant credibility to your claim. The line of thought would be, "If this candidate was able to navigate the rigorous hiring process at these other firms and they're prepared to compensate them so generously, we surely can't afford to lose such a valuable hire."

Try to synchronize the process so that all your offers are on the table around the same time, compelling companies to propose their best offers. Maintaining a positive attitude throughout the process is crucial. Justify your reasoning behind every decision.

Make use of the "mirroring" technique: echoing the last few words spoken by the other party. This method stimulates the other person to continue the conversation and divulge more information, which could be beneficial during negotiations. Posing open-ended questions that don't necessitate a "yes" or "no" response can be useful. They afford the other party a sense of control and often elicit valuable information.

Being ready to walk away is another powerful tactic in any negotiation, not just for job offers. It's important to remember that while you might really want a particular job, you should not feel obliged to accept an offer that doesn't meet your needs or expectations. If negotiations aren't going in your favor and you believe the offer isn't reflecting your worth, you need to be prepared to walk away. Doing so can actually increase your perceived value and may lead the company to reconsider its offer. This should not be used as a bluff, however. Only imply that you're ready to walk away if you genuinely are.

Negotiation is an art and requires practice. The more you do it, the better you get. Don't be afraid to practice these techniques in lower-stakes situations to build your confidence and hone your skills.

Learning, Earning or Leaving

Here's a simple guideline to evaluate each of your job opportunities: Focus on learning, earning or choosing to leave.

Learning: Nurturing growth and self-improvement

No matter your line of work, an essential element of any professional journey is to constantly seek out learning opportunities.

- **Skill enhancement:** Refining your analytical thinking, bettering your communication prowess or becoming proficient in new technology are examples of skill enhancement. The constant pursuit of skill enhancement not only boosts your work efficiency but also increases your self-assuredness and professional capacity. This paves the way for new pathways and chances for progression.

- **Broadening your knowledge:** Knowledge indeed reigns supreme in the business world. Staying informed about industry trends, being aware of market behavior and gaining a solid grasp of your area of expertise are vital to professional advancement. Expanding your knowledge reservoir can improve your problem-solving skills, foster innovation and enable you to make well-informed decisions.

- **Building competencies:** Learning also encompasses diversifying your competencies by gaining new capabilities. For instance, if your profession is software engineering, you might want to venture into blockchain technology or artificial intelligence. The development of new competencies keeps you agile and relevant in a fast-paced professional environment.

Earning: Utilizing skills for wealth creation

If you're not gaining substantial knowledge, it's essential that you're at least receiving considerable monetary benefits.

- **Compensation based on value:** It's crucial to ensure that your earnings reflect the value you bring to the organization. Negotiate for competitive compensation packages that accurately represent your contributions to your workplace. Understand your market worth and negotiate in accordance.

- **Professional progression:** The earning phase also involves ascending the career ladder. Utilize your skills and competencies to aim for roles and opportunities that offer increased responsibilities and, subsequently, higher earnings. This progression could involve promotions, lateral moves or even the establishment of your own business.

Leaving: Charting new paths for superior opportunities

If you find you're not acquiring fresh skills or reaping a satisfactory income, it can be an indication to move on.

- **Recognizing the need for change:** The inaugural step is realizing that your current role is neither rewarding nor lucrative. This could stem from several reasons such as a death of progression opportunities, stagnant income, an unhealthy workplace culture or personal discontent with your duties. It's critical to candidly assess your situation and feelings.

- **Exploring alternatives:** Upon recognizing the need for change, initiate your search for other prospects that better resonate with your career objectives and financial targets. This might involve exploring different sectors, roles, organizations or even self-owned ventures. Ensure that your skills, passions and long-term ambitions are central to this process.

- **Charting the transition:** Change, even for the better, is seldom straightforward, and shifting to a new role, sector or enterprise requires strategic planning. This encompasses financial management to navigate any phase of joblessness, obtaining new skills or refining existing ones if necessary and anticipating potential roadblocks that might surface during the shift.

- **Taking the plunge:** After conducting thorough research and preparation, it's time to take action on your decision. Whether this translates to tendering your resignation or launching your startup, it's imperative to make the transition with self-assuredness and a positive attitude.

Exiting a familiar scenario, even an unsatisfying one, can be intimidating. However, remember, the underlying principle of the "learn, earn or leave" philosophy is rooted in growth and advancement. If your growth is stunted, if your skills are undervalued or if your earnings don't match your worth, seeking change will pave the way to opportunities that offer enhanced learning, improved earnings and overall satisfaction.

Hopping Your Way to Success

When I began my professional journey, a young, green version of myself ardently believed in a simple equation for success. I was convinced that keeping my nose to the grindstone, persistently working hard without fuss, was the golden ticket to climbing the corporate ladder. Like a diligent soldier, I thought promotions, raises and greater income would naturally flow my way as the fruits of my labor. In the grand scheme of my imagination, my manager would sit in his ivory tower, constantly keeping an eye on my relentless endeavors, naturally rewarding me with the progression I sought. In this imaginary world, I played the role of the steadfast workhorse, tirelessly plowing through tasks, my efforts mirrored only by the increasing rings of coffee stains on my desk.

Days turned into weeks, and weeks into months, but the fairy-tale ending of my story seemed further and further away. My manager, contrary to my beliefs, did not seem to be the all-seeing eye, dutifully monitoring my efforts and itching to reward my hard work. Instead, he was preoccupied, caught up in the whirlwind of corporate pressures, deadlines and meetings. My tireless efforts, as it turned out, were only tiny blips on his radar. It was then that a bolt from the blue hit me: My path was not leading to the pot of gold at the end of the rainbow. It was a forewarning that made me realize the corporate world doesn't quite work in the simple, straightforward way I had imagined. My naive belief that hard work alone would lead to progression had been a misjudgment.

The light bulb moment came when I discovered the power of job hopping. It wasn't a disregard for loyalty, as some might think, but a strategic move in the vast chessboard of my career. By shifting roles and companies, I was able to learn new skills, meet new people and broaden my professional horizons. Each hop came with its challenges, but also its rewards, often in the form of increased responsibility and more importantly, better pay.

In previous eras, maintaining long tenure with a single organization was perceived as a mark of loyalty and stability. However, times have dramatically changed. Currently, the quickest strategy to accelerate your salary growth lies in job transitioning, also known as "job hopping." Let's dissect what job hopping entails. In essence, it refers to departing from your present job after a relatively short period (sometimes even less than a few years) to embark on a new role, usually within a different organization. It may appear counterintuitive at first, especially because societal norms often advocate loyalty as a virtue and prolonged tenure at one company as an indicator of stability, patience and dedication.

Nevertheless, empirical evidence suggests a contrary narrative. A study from the U.S. Bureau of Labor Statistics in 2019 revealed that employees who transition between jobs typically experience a more pronounced wage growth trajectory compared to those who remain stationary. This phenomenon, referred to as the "job hopping premium," is particularly prevalent among younger workers.

In today's fast-paced and dynamic job market, the rate at which salaries increase can far outpace the growth rate of salaries within a single organization. This is due to several factors including industry competition, technological advancements and the increased demand for specialized skills. Companies are often willing to pay a premium to attract the talent they need to stay competitive, especially in high demand fields. As a result, the market rate for these roles can surge significantly over a short period. Conversely, internal salary growth through promotions or annual raises, while significant, often cannot keep up with this external market rate growth. To put it simply, companies often prioritize budget constraints and salary structures over market trends. While they do offer raises and promotions, these are often bound by internal policies that limit the percentage increase in salary. As a result, loyal employees who stay with the same company for a long time may find that their salaries lag behind the market rate, despite regular raises and promotions. Meanwhile, external candidates can negotiate their pay based on the market rate rather than being constrained by a pre-existing salary structure. Therefore, changing jobs every few years can provide an opportunity to reset your salary closer to the market rate, particularly in high demand industries.

Using this strategy of strategic job hopping, I was able to skyrocket my annual income from a humble $74,000 to an impressive $500,000 in less than eight years. The magnitude of this increase might seem astounding, but it is a testament to the power of proactive career management and leveraging market dynamics to one's advantage.

Even when you're in a job you like, it's essential to maintain a posture of career preparedness. Changes in the workplace environment, such as downsizing, restructuring or layoffs, could happen unexpectedly. Market changes and shifts in company strategy can also lead to unforeseen circumstances affecting your job stability. Therefore, ensuring your professional documents are updated and honing your interview skills, even when you are happily employed, can provide a safety net and help prepare you for any eventuality. Maintaining an up-to-date résumé encourages self-reflection and professional growth. As you add new experiences and skills, you're likely to spot areas for development. Regular updates make the process less overwhelming than trying to remember all your accomplishments in one sitting. Interview skills are much like a muscle—the more you use them, the stronger they become. Regularly preparing for and simulating job interviews can help you become more comfortable with the process, even when you're not actively job hunting. The more you practice, the better you'll become at answering tough questions and promoting your skills and achievements. Staying aware of opportunities in the job market, even when you're content in your role, can provide valuable insights into industry trends and the demand for skills in your field. This can inform your professional development strategy, ensuring you keep your skills relevant.

While job hopping can be advantageous, it should be executed with a strategic approach. Excessive transitions within a brief span can potentially trigger concerns for prospective employers. If your tenure at multiple jobs is less than a year, be prepared to narrate compelling stories explaining the reasons. Striking the right balance is crucial: Remain in a role long enough to deliver substantial contributions and absorb meaningful lessons, but also recognize the right moment to advance forward.

Chapter 6

LIVING BELOW YOUR MEANS

The true key to financial prosperity and security isn't simply dictated by the size of your income, but by the amount of your earnings you successfully manage to save and invest. Living below your means is a cornerstone of financial health. It's about cultivating financial discipline, the kind that empowers you to distinguish between wants and needs, prioritizing the latter. It's about strategic spending, allocating funds in a way that ensures your present needs are met, while also safeguarding your future. By embracing frugality, you're not depriving yourself. Instead, you're setting yourself on a path of financial freedom and early retirement, offering you the priceless gift of time and peace of mind.

Frugality

Frugality is often unjustly associated with stinginess or deprivation, an undeserved negative reputation. Yet, the essence of frugality is far from self-deprivation or living in scarcity. It's time we redefine frugality, challenge these misconceptions and shed light on its true meaning.

At its heart, frugality is all about maximizing value, not merely trimming expenses. It revolves around resource optimization, making the best of what we have. Frugal individuals recognize that every purchase carries a cost that extends beyond the monetary value reflected on the price tag. Purchases can also exact costs in terms of space, time and energy, and lead to potential clutter and waste. Hence, frugality fosters mindful consumption habits. It prods us to pause and contemplate before making a purchase: "Is this item truly needed? Will it enhance my life in a significant way? Does its value justify the cost?"

Frugality is dependent on creativity and resourcefulness, allowing maximum extraction from current possessions, and is based on the principle of repair over replacement, repurposing of items and the minimization of waste. In essence, frugality is about prudent spending. It involves discerning between needs and wants, favoring purchases that provide the most value and sidestepping unnecessary expenditures. Comparison shopping, leveraging discounts and rewards, and exploring cost-efficient alternatives are all examples of frugality.

Frugality is a long-term approach that requires the consideration of the ramifications of our spending decisions. Practicing frugality compels us to contemplate the total cost of ownership, inclusive of maintenance, operation and disposal expenses.

However, frugality is not synonymous with always opting for the cheapest alternative. It underscores the significance of seeking value for money and investing in purchases that provide lasting benefits, endorsing a quality-over-quantity approach. A frugal individual endeavors to extract the best value for their money, contemplating factors such as durability, efficiency and usefulness in addition to price. They recognize the value of investing in high-quality products which, although they may demand a higher upfront cost, often deliver substantial long-term value.

Consider an instance in which a high-quality appliance like a refrigerator or washing machine requires a significant initial investment. The superior craftsmanship and materials used in these high-end products often ensure that they last longer and operate more efficiently, which can lead to substantial long-term savings. These appliances tend to be more durable, reducing the likelihood of frequent repairs and consequently, saving maintenance costs over the product's lifespan. Moreover, many such appliances are designed with energy efficiency as a prime consideration, which can lead to significant savings on utility bills.

Frugal individuals understand the concept of the "false economy," wherein the cheapest option might ultimately turn out to be more expensive in the long run. They are adept at making informed purchasing decisions that take into account both immediate costs and long-term value. Frugality, thus, is not about penny pinching but about making mindful, smart decisions that enhance our lives and financial well-being.

While frugality necessitates a primary focus on needs, it doesn't demand a complete eradication of wants. After all, life isn't just about survival, but about experiencing joy and fulfillment as well. Once we have adequately catered to our needs and set aside a portion of our resources for savings and investments, it's entirely acceptable to spend on our wants. However, it's crucial that such spending is conducted responsibly, without creating any financial strain.

Recognizing the difference between our wants and needs promotes a mindful approach to spending. It invites us to scrutinize our buying decisions, weigh their long-term impacts and steer clear of impulsive purchases. By practicing mindful spending, we can enhance the value we derive from our monetary resources and diminish the likelihood of experiencing post-purchase regret. Discerning between wants and needs enables us to resist the persuasive force of consumerism, which frequently pushes us toward desiring the latest gadgets or the trendiest fashion items. This resistance doesn't just benefit our financial health; it also fosters a more sustainable and less wasteful lifestyle.

Often, embracing frugality necessitates a paradigm shift from placing value on material possessions to cherishing experiences, relationships and personal development. Rather than seeking pleasure in acquiring new items, frugal individuals frequently find joy in simple, low-cost activities, like a nature walk, cooking a meal at home or spending quality time with loved ones. Contentment is rooted in gratitude for what we already possess. It involves acknowledging the worth of our belongings, relationships and experiences and cherishing the satisfaction they afford us. This gratitude checks our incessant desire for more and nurtures a feeling of sufficiency. While material possessions can offer convenience and comfort, they should not be regarded as the main source of joy or satisfaction in life. By choosing to spend less on material goods, we can redirect our resources, time, money and energy toward investing in ourselves, fostering our relationships and pursuing our passions. This might involve mastering a new skill, cultivating a hobby or dedicating quality time to loved ones.

At its core, frugality is about personal and financial empowerment. It's about taking the reins of your financial future, breaking away from the pattern of thoughtless consumption and aligning your expenditures with your values and aspirations. Frugality allows you to live within your means, evade debt, save for the future and attain financial peace of mind. In our consumer-oriented society, we are persistently bombarded with messages coaxing us to buy more and to own the newest, the biggest or the best. Adopting a frugal mindset provides resilience against these pressures, helping us identify these messages as what they truly are: marketing strategies aimed to instill discontent with our current possessions. Frugality is a lifestyle choice that involves making conscious decisions to live within our means, emphasizing value over quantity and fostering a sense of satisfaction and appreciation for what we possess. It's about attaining financial stability and tranquility and ultimately, leading a fulfilling and sustainable life.

Prosperity versus Reality

Once upon a time in the quaint suburban town of Cloverfield, the Anderson family was a quintessential portrait of middle-class Americana. Robert, a local car salesman, and Linda, a school teacher, lived comfortably with their two teenage children, Olivia and Michael, in a cozy home with a manicured lawn, white picket fence and their beloved golden retriever, Max. They were content, living a simple life filled with Friday night pizza dinners, Saturday soccer games and Sunday picnics in the park.

But things took a drastic turn when the Joneses moved into the sprawling mansion at the end of the lane. The Joneses were the epitome of opulence and extravagance, with a flashy lifestyle that the quiet town of Cloverfield had never seen. With their fancy cars, lavish parties and exotic vacations, they became the talk of the town, shifting the tranquility of the Andersons' world on its axis. Bit by bit, Robert and Linda found themselves ensnared in the allure of the Joneses' lifestyle. It started with small purchases, a new television to match the Joneses' home theater, a new barbecue grill as grand as the Joneses' and designer clothes to wear at community gatherings. Then came the luxury car that put a significant dent in their savings, followed by the lavish vacation that racked up a hefty amount on their credit cards, all to match the Joneses' affluent lifestyle. While they received admiring glances and complimentary remarks from their neighbors, the Anderson family's financial stability was crumbling under the weight of their new extravagant lifestyle. Bills started to pile up, credit card debts skyrocketed and tensions in their once peaceful home started to mount. The kids, Olivia and Michael, who were once happy and carefree, now felt the strain. Extracurricular activities and college funds had to be cut to cater to their parents' escalating desire to keep up with the Joneses. Olivia's dream of joining a prestigious dance academy was shattered and Michael had to let go of his aspirations of attending a renowned engineering university. As the financial strain escalated, so did the discord in the Anderson family. Robert and Linda, once a loving couple, now constantly bickered over finances. Olivia and Michael, once cheerful teenagers, were now mired in their parents' discontent. The story of the Anderson family serves as a powerful cautionary tale. Their futile pursuit of keeping up with the Joneses not only led them into financial ruin but also tore apart the once joyous structure of their family life. It is a reminder that happiness and contentment cannot be found in material possessions or the perception of others but in the peace and fulfillment of living within one's means.

Our society often misinterprets prosperity, associating it with material abundance, a luxury car, a sprawling mansion, the newest tech gadgets, high-end fashion, the enumeration is infinite. However, this interpretation of prosperity is often deceptive and creates an illusion. This mistaken belief can drive individuals toward an unsustainable lifestyle that exceeds their means.

The phrase "keeping up with the Joneses" springs from an inherent desire to project an image of success equivalent to or better than our peers or neighbors. This expression originates from a comic strip created by Arthur R. "Pop" Momand that depicted the socially ambitious McGinis family, who were perpetually struggling to match the lifestyle of their neighbors, the Joneses. Essentially, "keeping up with the Joneses" is a form of social comparison, in which we measure our value based on how we rank against others. This comparison could involve material possessions like real estate and vehicles or intangible aspects like professional positions and holiday destinations. Haven't we heard that comparison is the root of discontent? While a modest level of comparison can stimulate motivation and self-enhancement, it becomes problematic when it fuels extravagant consumption. The race to keep up with the Joneses can often lead to significant financial repercussions. It prompts people to live beyond their means, spending money they don't have on things they don't need, to uphold an image of affluence or success for people who, in reality, are indifferent about their lifestyle. This habit can generate a cycle of debt, as people resort to loans or credit cards to sustain their extravagant lifestyles. Over time, this can decimate your savings, hinder your financial progress and eventually lead to bankruptcy.

Besides financial repercussions, the persistent habit of comparing oneself with others can instigate stress, dissatisfaction and diminished self-worth. It breeds a mentality of insufficiency and discontent, in which no number of possessions or accomplishments seem enough because there's always someone who appears to have more. Societal and cultural norms heavily reinforce the urge to keep up with the Joneses. Media, advertisements and social networks exacerbate our sense of inadequacy and stimulate desires for material goods and lifestyle enhancements. These influences make it incredibly challenging for individuals to resist the temptation to compete materially with their peers. Acknowledging and resisting this pattern is a crucial step toward solid financial health and authentic contentment. The secret lies in concentrating on your own financial objectives and personal values, rather than striving to match or surpass what others possess.

The glamorous exhibition of wealth often conceals a precarious financial foundation. When we see individuals leading lavish lifestyles, driving the latest high-end vehicles, donned in designer apparel, residing in luxurious homes or jetting off on extravagant vacations, we usually associate such visible affluence with financial prosperity. However, this assumption can be misleading. A significant number of individuals who appear wealthy based on their spending patterns, may be barely making ends meet, with negligible savings or investments. They might be deep in debt, having borrowed substantially to fund their extravagant lifestyles. Beneath the glossy veneer, these individuals are suffocating under a mountain of debt, encompassing astronomical credit card bills, personal loans, vehicle installments or mortgage debts. Their incessant need to finance their lifestyles can engender a vicious cycle of debt that's challenging to escape. A minor financial hiccup, such as job loss or unexpected expenses, can trigger the collapse of their fragile financial edifice. Many who adopt a high-expenditure lifestyle neglect the importance of saving or investing, thereby forfeiting the advantages of compound interest and the potential for wealth accumulation over time. In essence, they are trading their future financial stability for present consumption. It's crucial to acknowledge the irony here: individuals with true wealth often don't feel compelled to flaunt it. Numerous affluent individuals worldwide are renowned for their frugality and discreet spending habits, recognizing that genuine wealth is not about ostentatious displays but about financial freedom, security and the power to make life-enhancing choices.

We exist in a society that typically associates prosperity with material acquisitions. However, real prosperity extends beyond material wealth. It encompasses financial stability, the liberty to make choices that enhance your life and the resilience to withstand financial turbulence. True prosperity also means planning for the future, which includes investing for retirement, establishing an emergency fund for unanticipated expenses and obtaining insurance to guard against unexpected eventualities. It's about creating a financial safety net that delivers peace of mind and ensures long-term financial wellness. Prosperity isn't purely a financial concept. It's about leading a balanced, fulfilling life, which incorporates maintaining good health, fostering meaningful relationships, pursuing personal growth and allocating time for relaxation and recreation. It's about overall well-being and life satisfaction, not merely the balance in your bank account or the brand of your vehicle.

As we navigate the path toward financial independence, it's vital to reevaluate our definition of prosperity. It isn't about ostentatious demonstrations of wealth or ceaselessly acquiring the latest products. Rather, it's about attaining financial stability, planning for the future and leading a fulfilling life. This shift in perspective is instrumental in fostering a healthier relationship with money and consumption. Frugality dovetails perfectly with this refined understanding of prosperity. It isn't about being miserly, but about consciously choosing to live within our means, prioritizing necessities and establishing a sustainable financial future. It's about recognizing that true wealth isn't attained through conspicuous consumption but through prudent financial management, smart investments and mindful living.

The Psychology of Spending

In the heart of New York City lived a young woman named Isabelle. Isabelle had everything going for her: a thriving career in tech, an apartment in the heart of Manhattan and a whirlwind social life.

However, beneath this facade of success, Isabelle had a problem that was slowly gnawing at her happiness, an inability to resist the siren call of retail therapy, marketing gimmicks and social pressures. Isabelle's problem started innocently enough. A spontaneous shopping spree after a tough day at work, the occasional impulse buy at the checkout counter. A sale here, a limited-time offer there, and she felt a thrill with each purchase. The bright, flashy ads she herself worked on drew her in and the appeal of "limited edition" and "exclusive" deals became irresistible.

In the beginning, it seemed like a harmless indulgence, a well-deserved reward for her hard work. But over time, the occasional indulgence morphed into a regular habit and soon, she found herself a prisoner of her own spending. Her social circle didn't help matters. Living in a city known for its materialistic allure, she found herself constantly under pressure to keep up with her friends' lifestyles. Every gathering was an occasion to flaunt the latest designer outfit or accessory and every conversation revolved around vacations to exotic locales or fine dining experiences. Slowly, her credit card bills began to pile up. Isabelle found herself juggling multiple debts, the high interest rates compounding her financial woes. The once enjoyable shopping excursions now filled her with dread and each "limited-time" offer seemed like a trap. The breaking point came when she could no longer afford her monthly rent and found herself facing the threat of eviction. It was then that she realized the gravity of her situation. The shiny items she'd accumulated seemed to mock her, standing as reminders of her reckless spending.

Comprehending the psychology underlying our spending habits can provide valuable insights into our financial conduct and assist us in cultivating healthier fiscal habits. Our expenditure patterns are influenced by an amalgamation of inherent and external factors, spanning our individual beliefs and emotions, societal norms and marketing ploys. This section delves further into these psychological facets, illuminating why we tend to spend the way we do and how we can make more informed financial choices.

A paramount psychological factor influencing our spending patterns is the craving for immediate gratification. The concept of instant gratification stems from our basic survival instincts. In the era of our ancestors, instant access to resources, such as food or shelter, could delineate the fine line between survival and extinction. However, in the context of our modern consumer society, these instincts can often lead us down the wrong path. In the current digital age, we are incessantly exposed to advertisements designed to tap into our desire for immediate rewards. Marketers fully comprehend that presenting us with a chance to satisfy a want instantly can override our rational judgment, resulting in impulsive buying decisions. The digital economy has revolutionized the ease and immediacy of spending money. With the advent of online shopping and credit cards, the act of purchasing items no longer necessitates the physical exchange of money, further distancing the purchasing act from its consequent impact on our bank balances. This often culminates in spending more than we had initially planned, potentially leading to chronic debt if not judiciously managed. Reflect on how tempting it is to click the "buy now" button while casually browsing through an online store, even if the item isn't necessary. Contemplate the allure of upgrading your smartphone each time a new model is released, regardless of the fact that your current device is functioning perfectly well. These instances exemplify how our yearning for instant gratification can precipitate poor financial decisions.

Social pressure is another potent driver of spending behavior. Our inherent desire for social approval and a sense of belonging can occasionally supersede fiscal wisdom, prompting decisions that are not in our best financial interests. We previously explored the perilous implications of the "keeping up with the Joneses" phenomenon. Platforms like Instagram often present a glorified portrayal of life, replete with exotic holidays, gourmet dining and high-end fashion, rendering our own lives seemingly humdrum by comparison. This can incite the urge to exceed our budget to emulate these ostentatious lifestyles. Societal expectations can coax us into splurging on items we don't genuinely need or desire. For instance, one might feel compelled to host an opulent wedding, largely due to social pressure, even though a smaller, more intimate celebration might have been preferable. It's vital to strive for a lifestyle that aligns with your budget and personal values, as opposed to one that's dictated by societal expectations or the lifestyles of others.

Some of the most intellectually gifted individuals dedicate their lives to persuading you to buy their company's offerings. Our consumption patterns are considerably swayed by the tactical maneuvers of marketing professionals. Vendors and advertisers frequently deploy complex psychological tactics to spur spending, ranging from intelligent store layouts and pricing strategies to personalized advertising and limited-period offers that induce a sense of urgency.

Retailers meticulously plan store layouts to subconsciously guide your shopping behavior. For instance, they may position high-priced items at eye level, relying on the tendency of consumers to grab items within easy reach, while placing less expensive goods on lower shelves. Another cunning tactic is the use of price points, such as tagging an item at $9.99 rather than $10. The psychological impact of this minor price difference is surprising, making the item appear significantly cheaper than it truly is.

Additionally, stores strategically locate candies, magazines and other impulse items near the checkout counters. This practice takes advantage of the moments when customers are waiting in line, often leading to impromptu purchases. The rise of data analytics has empowered personalized advertising to become a formidable tool for swaying spending behavior. Retailers can now customize their marketing messages to individual consumer behaviors, which enhances the probability of purchases. Limited time offers and flash sales are additional strategies used to create a sense of urgency, propelling consumers to buy instantly due to the fear of losing out on a great deal. Phrases like "while stocks last" or "limited supply" are cleverly used to augment this urgency effect.

Emotions play a pivotal role in our spending decisions, with "retail therapy" being a prime example. This phrase refers to the practice of indulging in shopping to alleviate stress or negative emotions. During times of tension, melancholy or even overwhelming joy, we may resort to shopping as a form of emotional palliative or celebration. While this might grant a fleeting sense of relief, it often leads to spontaneous and potentially unnecessary purchases. For instance, following a particularly taxing day at work, the temptation to unwind by going on a shopping spree or ordering an extravagant item online can be enticing.

Equipping ourselves with knowledge about these psychological triggers enables us to make deliberate choices and resist harmful spending influences. Recognizing the allure of instant gratification can help us nurture patience and prioritize long-term financial objectives over immediate desires. Understanding the sway of social pressure can propel us to make choices anchored in our needs and fiscal health, rather than societal expectations. Being privy to marketing strategies can aid us in making informed decisions that are not swayed by slick advertising, but steered by our personal necessities and financial capabilities. Acknowledging the nexus between emotions and spending can foster healthier coping mechanisms, mitigating the chances of impulsive or emotional expenditure.

The Value of Your Time

Growing up, my father was a staunch disciple of the penny-pinching gospel. He was the kind of man who would drive an extra ten miles to save three cents on a gallon of gas. He believed every penny saved was a penny earned, an ethos he imbibed from his own parents and his poverty-filled youth.

One particular incident that stands out in my memory involves a large furniture set we had ordered. The set was perfect, a beautiful mahogany dining table with matching chairs, a stunning piece that my mother had dreamt of owning for a long time. The catch, however, was the exorbitant shipping fee. Determined not to pay a penny more than he thought was necessary, my dad decided that we would pick up the furniture ourselves. But this wouldn't involve simply borrowing a neighbor's truck or renting a convenient moving van. No, my dad insisted on locating the cheapest rental truck available within a fifty-mile radius. That day, I remember waking up before dawn, sharing a quick breakfast of cold cereal with my dad as we looked at the day's task ahead. We drove to the outskirts of town, to a grungy rental place that had the cheapest deal. We had to wait for hours because the truck wasn't ready, it needed a part replaced. As the day rolled on, my stomach growled with hunger and my eyes grew heavy from the lack of sleep. I looked over at my dad, his silhouette bathed in the harsh neon light of the truck rental office. He was tired too; I could see it in the lines etched on his face. But he was stubborn, his resolve as unyielding as the rusted metal trucks around us. By the time we got the truck and drove to the furniture store, loaded up our new dining set and made our way back home, the sun was setting. Our whole day had been consumed by this endeavor, all to save a few dollars on shipping fees.

A significant aspect of frugality that is often overlooked is the importance of time. Time, unlike money, is a finite resource that cannot be replenished once it has been used. Recognizing the value of our time can greatly influence our decision-making process, affecting not only our spending habits but also our choices in the workplace and our overall lifestyle priorities.

A helpful first step is determining your hourly wage, whether your pay is hourly or salaried. To do this, identify your net earnings for a specific period, such as a week or a month. Net earnings are your take-home pay after accounting for taxes and other deductions. If your income is salaried, divide this net amount by the number of hours worked within that period. This exercise is essential not just for hourly employees, but also for salaried individuals to understand their true hourly wage. In determining your hourly wage, it's vital to consider all the time you dedicate to your work. This includes not only the hours you're officially "at work," but also time spent commuting, responding to emails outside of work hours or even contemplating work during your off-hours. All these hours invested in your job should be factored into your calculations.

When you understand the worth of your time, you're better equipped to evaluate the costs and benefits of various options. Let's consider a few scenarios: Imagine an appliance in your home malfunctions. You could invest several hours trying to fix it yourself or you could hire a professional to handle the repair. If you're leaning toward the DIY approach, take the time to estimate the amount of time it would take and consider the monetary worth of that time. It might be more cost effective to employ a professional and devote your time to tasks more in line with your skills or tasks that provide greater satisfaction. What if you had a chance to save money by driving across town to a less expensive store? While the savings might be immediately apparent, don't overlook the value of the time spent commuting. It might be more reasonable to save time by shopping at the closer, albeit slightly pricier, store.

This principle extends to your professional life as well. Understanding your time's value can assist you in making decisions about working overtime, making a career move or launching a business. Employees often struggle with deciding whether to accept overtime work. On the surface, it appears an opportunity to earn more. However, when viewed through the time value lens, the decision may not be so straightforward. For example, if the pay for overtime doesn't substantially exceed your calculated hourly wage, the extra hours might not be worth the sacrifice, particularly if it comes at the expense of relaxation, personal pursuits or time with family. If you're considering a career transition, think about how your time's value may change in the potential new role. A higher salary may be enticing, but if it demands significantly longer hours, the increase in your effective hourly wage might not be as considerable as initially assumed. For those considering starting a business, understanding the value of your time is essential. As an entrepreneur, you'll likely take on many roles, especially in the early stages. Therefore, you need to strategically allocate your time to high value tasks that directly influence your business's growth. Tasks with lower value, if possible, should be delegated or outsourced.

A common pitfall when valuing time is underestimating the significance of leisure time. The adage "time is money" can inadvertently prompt us to perceive every moment as a potential moneymaking opportunity, resulting in the disregard or undervaluation of non-working hours. However, recognizing and appreciating the true worth of leisure time can greatly enhance our overall well-being and life satisfaction. Leisure time is a crucial opportunity for rest and revitalization. After a demanding week of work, taking time to relax allows both body and mind to recover. This period of rest isn't merely a luxury; it's an essential requirement. Overworking can result in burnout, diminished productivity and health complications. By valuing your leisure time, you acknowledge the necessity of rest for maintaining your health and sustaining long-term productivity.

Similarly, the quality time shared with family and friends is priceless. It nurtures relationships, creates memories and delivers emotional support. While it may not have a direct financial return in the traditional sense, the subjective value of robust personal relationships is incalculable. Striking a balance between work and leisure is essential for maintaining mental well-being.

Appreciating the value of your time, in both monetary and personal terms, is key to leading a frugal lifestyle. By understanding how much your time is worth, you can make informed decisions about work and leisure, allowing you to determine whether it's more economical to do a task yourself or hire someone else to do it, for example. When evaluating a job offer, consider not just the salary, but the required hours, commuting time and stress levels, ensuring that the pay aligns with the time and effort you'll be investing. Assessing the monetary and personal value of time allows you to find a balance between financial considerations and personal fulfillment. The monetary value of your time can guide you toward making sound financial decisions, while the personal value of your time can ensure these decisions don't infringe upon your personal well-being, relationships and life enjoyment. This equilibrium is key to sustaining a rewarding and fulfilling lifestyle.

By grasping the true value of your time, you are better prepared to prioritize and distribute it effectively. You can distinguish between what's important and what's not, between what warrants your time and what doesn't. This enables you to direct your time toward activities that deliver the most benefits, be they financial, personal or emotional. This perspective encourages more mindful time management, leading to a more rewarding and fulfilling life. You become more productive, more focused and less likely to squander time on inconsequential activities. You're more inclined to invest time in activities that bring you happiness, promote personal growth and contribute to your financial goals. It isn't solely about monetary gain; it's about achieving life satisfaction, facilitating personal growth and, ultimately, forging a path to financial independence.

Credit Cards

When I was a software engineer living in the bustling city of San Francisco, I quickly realized that life could get expensive. I loved to travel, but the escalating costs were always a barrier. That was until my friend told me about harnessing the power of credit cards for rewards. My curiosity piqued, I decided to dive deeper into this intriguing world of sign-up bonuses, rewards and points. Fast forward a couple of years, with careful use of my credit cards, I amassed an abundance of reward points. These points turned into flight tickets and hotel stays that didn't cost me a penny. From visiting relatives in China to meandering through the streets of Japan, I got to travel without straining my wallet, thanks to my credit card rewards. But the perks of responsible credit card use didn't stop at travel. There was this one time I ordered a high-end gaming computer, only to find I had been sent a defective piece of hardware. With the seller refusing to acknowledge the issue or process a refund, I was at my wit's end. However, my credit card's consumer protection policy proved to be a lifesaver. I was able to dispute the transaction and recoup my money, a protection that would have been missing had I paid with cash or debit. In another instance, my brand-new bike fell apart within weeks of purchase. Again, my credit card's purchase protection came to my rescue, covering the cost of repairs. Credit cards, when used strategically, can offer more than just a convenient way to pay. They can offer lucrative rewards, cash back, purchase protection and aid in credit score building, among other advantages.

A credit score is a numerical expression derived from an analysis of your credit files, intended to represent your creditworthiness. Credit scores, as calculated by FICO, range from 300 to 850. Generally, a higher score is indicative of a healthier credit status. A score of 650 is viewed as 'good', while a score of 800 or above is considered 'excellent'. For most credit card approvals, a score of 700 is usually sufficient, although some premium cards might necessitate a higher score.

Becoming an authorized user (AU) can potentially improve your credit score if the primary cardholder has a good credit history. For example, if you're an AU on a parent's credit card with a lengthy and positive credit history, this can boost your score. However, it's important to remember that any negative actions on the part of the primary cardholder can also affect your score. When trying to help a family member build credit, you can make them an AU on your card, but avoid becoming an AU on their card. Moreover, any debt accumulated is your responsibility, so trust is paramount when granting AU status. Numerous websites offer free access to your credit score. Increasingly, credit card companies also provide this service either on their monthly statements or through their online platforms.

Using a credit card responsibly can help build or improve your credit score, which is essential for securing loans, renting an apartment or even getting a job. Making your credit card payments on time consistently is one of the best ways to build a positive credit history. Payment history is the most heavily weighted factor in calculating credit scores. Late payments, including those for medical bills or other services, can significantly dent your score. Credit utilization is the amount of your available credit that you're using at any given time. A lower credit utilization rate can positively impact your credit score. It's generally recommended to keep your utilization below 30% of your total credit limit. This is why 'maxing out your cards' is discouraged, as it signals potential risk to the bank that you might default on your balance. The longer you hold a credit card and use it responsibly, the more it can contribute to a healthy credit score.

The biggest advantage of using credit cards is the opportunity to earn rewards and cash back on your purchases. These rewards can effectively reduce your expenses and give you additional perks, enhancing the value you get from your spending. Certain credit cards, often known as travel credit cards, reward you with points or miles for each dollar you spend. These points or miles can then be redeemed for a variety of travel-related expenses, providing great value if you frequently travel. For every purchase you make, you'll earn a specific number of points or miles. The earning rate can vary widely depending on the card and the type of purchase. For example, you might earn more points per dollar for travel or dining expenses than for other types of purchases. You can redeem your accumulated points or miles for a variety of rewards. These might include airline tickets, hotel stays, car rentals and even travel experiences. Some cards also allow points or miles to be converted to gift cards, merchandise or cash back. Often, credit cards provide additional travel benefits such as free checked bags, priority boarding, airport lounge access and travel insurance. Understanding these benefits and using them strategically can enhance your travel experience. Search for "credit card churning" forums to maximize these rewards.

Cash back credit cards reward you with a percentage of your spending in the form of cash rewards. This simple and straightforward reward system can save you significant money on your everyday purchases. Each time you make a purchase with a cash back credit card, you earn a certain percentage back. The rate can vary from 1% to as high as 5% or more, depending on the card and the type of purchase. Some cards offer a flat rate on all purchases, while others offer higher rates in specific categories like groceries, gas or dining. The cash back you earn can be used in a variety of ways. You could apply it as a statement credit to reduce your credit card bill or you might choose to redeem it for gift cards or deposits into a bank account. Some cards may even allow you to invest your cash back into a retirement or brokerage account. Whether you're earning points, miles or cash back, these rewards programs can provide a substantial financial benefit. They're a key reason why using a credit card responsibly can be a smart financial move. Chase Freedom Unlimited® is a great card if you're interested in getting cash back.

Before applying for your credit card, remember that browsing through credit card websites might not always yield the best signup bonuses. Occasionally, banks might temporarily enhance their point bonuses to lure new customers or during specific seasons. It's quite common for individuals to rush into signing up for a card, only to discover a better signup bonus later. While some banks like Chase might allow you to claim the extra points from a superior offer, others like Amex are known to issue courtesy points instead of matching. However, some banks like Citi might outright decline such requests. Be smart and invest a bit of time in researching the best signup bonus. A brief 15 minute research could be the difference between hundreds and thousands of points.

If you're contemplating applying for an airline or hotel card, your first step should be visiting the company website and setting up a loyalty account because of the potential for better offers, ease of application and because some credit card offers are exclusive to existing members. Never sign up for in-store credit cards (with Costco and Amazon being notable exceptions if you shop at either heavily).

In addition to the lucrative sign-up bonuses, many credit cards provide purchase protection, which is a type of insurance for items purchased with the card. Purchase protection can cover lost, stolen or damaged goods for a certain period after the purchase, usually 90 to 120 days. This can provide peace of mind, especially for big-ticket items. Some cards also offer extended warranties, price protection and return protection. Credit cards often come with additional perks like travel insurance, rental car insurance and access to special events or discounts. Some also offer zero fraud liability, meaning you won't be held responsible for unauthorized charges made on your card. You should get into the habit of paying for everything with your credit card for this perk alone. American Express® has the best customer service in my experience.

It's important to note, however, that the benefits of credit cards come with the responsibility of careful usage. To maximize the benefits and avoid pitfalls such as high-interest rates or debt, always aim to pay your balance in full each month, spend within your means and utilize the rewards and protections that your card provides. Credit cards can be your financial allies, provided you utilize them with wisdom and responsibility.

The Hedonic Treadmill

The hedonic treadmill, also referred to as "hedonic adaptation," is a psychological concept that describes how humans maintain a fairly consistent level of happiness, regardless of significant positive or negative events or increased consumption. In terms of wealth, it encapsulates the idea that as our income expands, our desires and expectations simultaneously grow. Consequently, material progress or success doesn't always translate into a sustained boost in happiness.

As we accumulate more wealth, upscale our homes or upgrade our vehicles, we may experience a transient spike in happiness. However, this emotional uplift is typically ephemeral. For instance, imagine receiving a substantial raise. In celebration, you buy a luxury car you've always coveted. Initially, the vehicle provides immense joy: The plush leather seats, the effortless handling and the admiring looks from onlookers all boost your sense of happiness. As time passes, however, what was once seen as luxurious and thrilling becomes the new norm. The initial delight of driving the luxury vehicle diminishes. Now, your gaze is set on an even more luxurious car or a larger home, under the impression that these will replenish your dwindling happiness. This cycle exemplifies the hedonic treadmill, a ceaseless chase for happiness in the next significant acquisition, only to discover that the thrill wanes over time. While you're in pursuit of these fleeting doses of happiness, your financial resources are increasingly channeled away from long-term wealth accumulation toward short-term gratification.

Breaking free from the grips of the hedonic treadmill isn't a quick fix, but a continuous commitment to deciphering what genuinely fuels our joy. It commences with awareness and education, the acknowledgement that the excitement triggered by novel possessions or status enhancements is often fleeting, keeping us in a continual, stressful chase for the next impressive achievement. Identifying this cycle is the inaugural step. We must comprehend that although acquiring a grander house, a newer car or the latest technological gadget may induce a brief spell of satisfaction, it's typically transient. As adaptable beings, we quickly acclimate to new circumstances, soon taking them for granted, thus diluting the initial thrill.

The next phase entails reshaping our happiness sources. Switching our focus from material assets to the nonmaterial facets of life can significantly influence our long-term happiness and satisfaction. Concentrate on deriving joy from nonmaterial life aspects, such as relationships, personal development, health and experiences. Robust social connections—with family, friends or community—are consistently reported as major contributors to happiness. Activities like learning a new skill, pursuing a hobby or enhancing physical fitness provide a sense of accomplishment and elevate our self-esteem over the long haul.

Fostering meaningful relationships imparts a sense of belonging and support that outlasts the exhilaration of a new acquisition. Studies indicate that these elements contribute more to our enduring happiness than material possessions. We should cultivate gratitude for what we possess, focus on nonmaterial joy sources and ensure our expenditures align with what genuinely provides us with lasting happiness. It's about understanding that enduring happiness seldom stems from what we possess, but rather from who we are, what we engage in and how we interpret the world around us.

From an economic standpoint, the key to breaking free from the hedonic treadmill involves warding off lifestyle inflation. Lifestyle inflation, or lifestyle creep, refers to a scenario in which your expenditure scales up in tandem with your income growth. It's a concept closely tied to the hedonic treadmill, symbolizing our endless yearning for more lavish, superior and abundant acquisitions. Keeping lifestyle inflation under control is paramount for achieving financial freedom and extricating ourselves from the influence of the hedonic treadmill. Upon receiving a pay increase or additional funds, it's enticing to splurge on luxuries, enhance your living standards or rationalize purchasing items that aren't truly necessary. While there's nothing wrong with occasional indulgence, issues arise when these costs become a regular expectation. If your lifestyle standards keep adjusting upward with each income increase, you end up curtailing or potentially annihilating your capacity to save and invest for the future.

Avoiding lifestyle inflation doesn't mean you should never uplift your living standards. It advocates a more deliberate approach to expenditure and saving. Regard your savings and investments as obligatory expenses. Whenever your income surges, elevate the amount you're setting aside for the future. This "pay yourself first" philosophy promotes treating savings as a nonnegotiable outlay. Be vigilant of your spending patterns. Constantly question the necessity of a purchase and its contribution to your long-term objectives.

The hedonic treadmill can often incite choices that are financially unwise and emotionally unsatisfying. The relentless chase for newer, grander and superior possessions can deplete our financial resources and leave us in a state of perpetual discontent. However, identifying and understanding this cycle can clear the path for more mindful decisions that align with our genuine financial and personal well-being. Financial independence isn't solely about possessing the funds to buy anything we desire. It's about having the liberty to make choices that resonate with our values, devoid of undue financial pressure. Evading the snare of the hedonic treadmill enables us to save and invest more, propelling our journey toward financial independence. By living within our means, prioritizing necessities over desires and investing judiciously, we can construct a financial foundation that supports this liberty.

Instead of pursuing immediate gratification, concentrating on long-term objectives provides a sense of purpose and direction. Whether it's early retirement, home ownership, education funding or backing a cause we believe in, these objectives can inspire us to make financial decisions that support our long-term vision rather than transient pleasure. A critical takeaway from understanding the hedonic treadmill is the recognition that material possessions don't guarantee enduring happiness. Awareness of the hedonic treadmill aids us in making more informed spending decisions. We become more cognizant of why we wish to make a purchase: is it a necessity, a means to impress others or a pursuit of transitory happiness? This mindfulness assists us in differentiating between needs and wants, curbing unnecessary expenses and augmenting our ability to save and invest.

End Goals

I remember how it all started: fresh out of college, enthusiastic and bursting with ambition. I had dreams of climbing the corporate ladder, of rising to the top of the corporate world. I hopped from job to job; each step was an upgrade to a higher position, a bigger company, a better salary. It was the kind of trajectory many would covet, but deep down, something didn't sit right. The drawn out work weeks, the constant chase for approval and the ceaseless drive for perfection began to weigh heavy on my soul. I was in a perpetual state of stress and my health was deteriorating. My personal life was nonexistent. I didn't have time to call my family, let alone visit them. The aspiration for success had eclipsed everything else. I was a hamster in the wheel, running tirelessly but going nowhere.

One day, everything changed. It was an ordinary Tuesday, a long day of meetings and deadlines when I got the call. My grandmother, the woman who had raised me, who taught me to value family and love above all, had passed away. It was an unforgiving wake-up call. I realized, in the worst way possible, that I had lost sight of what mattered most to me. Her passing made me stop and think. Why was I working so tirelessly for these faceless companies? Why was I sacrificing my happiness, my health and my relationships for a job that would replace me in a heartbeat? What was it all for? In my heart, I knew my number one priority had always been family. But somehow, along the way, I had lost sight of this truth. It was time for a reset. I started reevaluating my life goals. I decided to chase after a different dream, one that valued time over money, relationships over promotions and happiness over material possessions. I set my sights on escaping the rat race as quickly as possible. The journey was tough and it took a lot of discipline and determination. But every sacrifice, every cutback and every hard decision was worth it when I considered the end goal.

Maintaining a focus on the ultimate objective is a crucial facet of effective frugal living. The expedition toward financial independence can often feel formidable, marked by daily choices and enduring sacrifices. Nevertheless, possessing a lucid image of your aspirations can function as a lighthouse, helping you navigate the intricate path and keeping your drive and enthusiasm alive for your aspiration to retire early, break free from the relentless cycle of work and attain financial sovereignty. This constitutes the "why" to your financial "what."

The SMART framework is a popular tool used in goal setting that transforms vague or broad objectives into concrete, achievable targets. The acronym SMART stands for specific, measurable, achievable, relevant and time-bound, each of which represents a key attribute of an effective goal.

Specific: Goals should be well-defined and clear, providing a distinct picture of what you aim to achieve. A specific goal addresses the who, what, where, when and why. It leaves no room for ambiguity or confusion. For example, instead of setting a goal like "I want to get fit," a specific goal could be "I want to be able to run a 5k marathon in 30 minutes within six months."

Measurable: Goals should be quantifiable to track progress and determine when the goal has been met. The inclusion of measurable criteria helps maintain motivation and allows for adjustments if needed. For instance, a measurable goal could be "I want to save $10,000 for a home down payment by the end of the year."

Achievable: Goals should be realistic and attainable, not so challenging that they become demotivating or set you up for failure. While a goal should push you out of your comfort zone, consider your resources and abilities. If a goal is set too high, it may be difficult to invest the effort required to meet it, leading to frustration and resignation.

Relevant: Goals should align with your broader life objectives and personal or professional values. This relevance ensures that achieving your goal brings you closer to your larger aims and keeps you engaged and committed. For instance, if your broad aim is to achieve financial independence, a relevant goal could be "I will cut my monthly expenses by 15% to increase my savings rate."

Time-bound: Goals should have a defined timeline or deadline, creating a sense of urgency that can motivate action. This time frame provides a clear end point to work toward and helps to prioritize the goal. For example, "I will learn Spanish to an intermediate level in one year" has a set timeline that encourages consistent progress.

The journey to financial independence is not a sprint; it's a marathon. It requires patience, perseverance and a strong commitment to your financial goals. By employing the SMART framework to define your goals, you're effectively laying a strong foundation for your journey, one that is firmly rooted in clarity, focus and intentionality. Your frugal lifestyle becomes more than just a means to an end; it becomes a fulfilling journey of self-discovery, growth and lasting financial freedom.

Visualization is a powerful tool that can bring your financial goals to life. This technique entails creating a mental or physical depiction of your desired outcomes, rendering your aspirations more concrete and palpable. Visualization operates on the tenet that our brains react robustly to visual stimuli. By visually embodying your objectives, you can keep them at the forefront of your consciousness and inspire your subconscious to remain focused on accomplishing them.

One effective method of visualization is creating a vision board. A vision board is a compilation of images, phrases or symbols signifying your ambitions and hopes. In the context of financial goals, this may comprise pictures of your dream home, a relaxing hammock on a beach or a stunning sunset. Essentially, it can include anything symbolizing tranquility, relaxation and the freedom of retirement. This visual depiction can serve as a constant reminder of your aspirations, strengthening your commitment to your financial voyage.

Another efficient visualization strategy involves the use of written affirmations. Declaring your financial targets in unambiguous, optimistic, present tense statements can aid in internalizing your goals and sustaining a positive mindset. You might write phrases like, "I am confidently investing 50% of my income each month," or "I am financially secure and debt-free." Although it might sound cliché, it's worth noting that your mindset governs your actions and these actions, in turn, lay the groundwork for your future.

The celebration of milestones plays a pivotal role in maintaining motivation on your journey to financial independence. The expedition toward your financial goals, not just the end point, significantly contributes to your overall sense of accomplishment. Milestones function as signposts, reflecting the distance you've traversed. Every stride forward, irrespective of its size, signifies progress. Honoring these moments underscores the value of the journey, reinforcing your dedication to the process. Each celebratory instance triggers positive emotions, forming a strong psychological connection between your efforts and the subsequent rewards. This gratifying feedback loop can sustain motivation and encourage you to persist with your financial plans, even amidst hurdles.

How you choose to mark these milestones can be customized to your preferences. These markers might entail a small personal reward, a communal celebration with family or friends or simply taking a moment to acknowledge your progress. The crucial element is ensuring the celebration aligns with your principles and does not deviate from your financial goals. Be it paying off a portion of your debt, achieving a savings target or adhering to your budget over a specified period, even small victories carry weight. They build momentum, leading to larger successes. The trajectory toward financial triumph is seldom linear and includes occasional setbacks. However, celebrating milestones aids in maintaining a positive outlook and reinforces the sense of progression.

The power of keeping the end goal in mind cannot be overstated when it comes to frugal living. It imbues your journey with purpose, directs your decision-making process, fuels your motivation and enables you to track your progress toward financial freedom. It transforms the journey from a mere attempt to save money into a fulfilling voyage toward a future marked by financial stability and freedom.

Chapter 7

INVEST
THE DIFFERENCE

You might find yourself wondering: how do we put our hard-earned money to work, yielding consistent returns without taking on excessive risk? How can we channel our savings toward early retirement and financial independence? The answer to this, surprisingly, is much simpler than it appears. As discussed earlier, a reliable strategy involves investment in a low-cost S&P 500 index fund, such as $VOO, but the question remains: why? This chapter will explore the fundamentals of investing and explain why entrusting your funds to the American stock market is a smart move.

Why You Need to Invest

Stagnant money is equivalent to depreciating money. If your wealth isn't appreciating, it's losing value. This is because the danger of inflation is always looming. Inflation represents the gradual increase in the price of goods and services over time, an economic reality that reduces the purchasing power of money. To put it simply, as inflation increases, every dollar you own buys a smaller percentage of a good or service. This doesn't mean that the physical amount of money you have decreases, but rather, what you can buy with that money decreases. If your money isn't growing at a rate equal to or exceeding inflation, you're effectively becoming poorer without spending a cent. Investing offers a shield against inflation, as it provides the opportunity to earn returns that outpace the inflation rate, thereby preserving and potentially enhancing the buying power of your wealth.

Consider having $100 today. If the annual inflation rate is 2% (roughly in line with historical averages of many developed economies), you'd require $102 a year from now to purchase the same goods or services that $100 buys today. This reduction in the purchasing power of money is the quintessential characteristic of inflation.

To illustrate this more clearly, take the cost of a gallon of milk. If it's priced at $3 today, a 2% inflation rate would hike its cost to $3.06 next year. Over the span of years, such price escalations can substantially influence your living expenses.

Let's revisit that $100, now stashed in a savings account yielding a 0.5% annual interest, with inflation standing at 2%.

After a decade, your savings, courtesy of the annual interest, would inflate to roughly $105. However, with a 2% annual inflation rate over these ten years, your $100 would have depreciated to the point where you'd need about $122 to enjoy the same purchasing power you had at the start.

Fast forward another decade and your savings account would have grown to approximately $110, but due to inflation, you'd require about $149 to retain the same purchasing power as your original $100. Here's a table where the future value of $100 is calculated to show how much money you would need to maintain the same purchasing power today. The formula used was:

Future Value = Present Value × (1 + Inflation Rate)
Number of Years

Years into the future	2% inflation	3% inflation	4% inflation	5% inflation
5	$110.41	$115.93	$121.67	$127.63
10	$121.90	$134.39	$148.02	$162.89
15	$134.59	$155.80	$180.09	$207.89
20	$148.59	$180.61	$219.11	$265.33
25	$164.06	$209.38	$266.58	$338.64
30	$181.14	$242.73	$324.34	$432.19
35	$199.99	$281.39	$394.61	$551.60
40	$220.80	$326.20	$480.10	$704.00

Now, how do we combat this wealth-eroding adversary? The answer lies in investing. Investing allows your money to work for you, expanding its potential and shielding it from the relentless effects of inflation. When you invest, your money isn't just sitting idly by; it's being put to work, growing and generating returns. Assume that instead of saving, you had chosen to invest that $100 in a diversified portfolio of stocks, yielding an average annual return of 7%. In ten years, you'd find yourself with about $196 and in twenty years, your investment could have bloomed to approximately $386. Even after factoring in a 2% inflation rate (which would necessitate having $122 after 10 years and $149 after 20 years to preserve your purchasing power), it becomes evident that investing would not only help maintain, but also significantly boost, your purchasing power over time.

Investing Basics

Investing, in its simplest form, is the process of committing resources, typically monetary, today with the expectation of yielding a profitable return in the future. This future return may take different forms, such as an appreciation in the asset's original value, a consistent income stream generated by the asset or both. Investment serves as a fundamental tool in wealth creation and preservation, allowing your money to actively generate wealth for you, instead of you toiling to earn money. Compounding power, the ability for your investments to earn returns not only on the initial principal but also on the accumulated returns, accelerates wealth growth. Albert Einstein is often quoted as referring to this phenomenon as the "eighth wonder of the world." Over time, consistent and thoughtful investments, through the power of compounding, can accumulate into a significant fortune, making it an invaluable tool in wealth creation.

Contrary to some perceptions, investing is not an activity exclusive to the wealthy or those who possess financial expertise. Investing is a journey that anyone, regardless of their economic background or knowledge level, can embark upon. The key to successful investing doesn't lie in the size of your starting capital or an intricate understanding of complex financial instruments; rather, it is rooted in the grasp of fundamental principles; an early start; and maintaining a steady, unwavering approach. It's important not to let short-term market fluctuations drive your decisions. Establishing a regular investment habit, like setting aside a fixed amount each month, will serve you better in the long run. Even better is to automate that process so you don't have to think about it.

Investments come in varied forms, each possessing unique traits, associated risks and potential rewards. Let's dive into some fundamental financial principles along with the most popular types of investments.

Diversification

Diversification is an essential investment strategy, metaphorically akin to not putting all your eggs in a single basket. This tactic aims to mitigate the overall risk of your investment portfolio by distributing your capital across a diverse selection of assets, sectors, geographical regions or investment styles. By doing so, the underperformance of any particular investment has a minimized impact, shielding your portfolio from severe losses. Diversification's primary advantage is risk reduction, as a well-balanced portfolio is less prone to dramatic value fluctuations. Losses from underperforming investments can be counterbalanced by the gains from others, resulting in a smoother growth trajectory for your investment portfolio over time. Diversification allows you to tap into a wider range of opportunities, enabling you to capture returns whenever and wherever they arise. This approach not only diffuses risk but also enhances potential rewards.

Risk and reward

Risk and reward are the two pivotal facets of investing that exist in a delicate balance: as the potential reward escalates, so does the associated risk and vice versa. This interplay forms the foundation of the investment arena and drives the decisions made by investors of all skill levels. In investment parlance, risk refers to the uncertainty surrounding the returns an investment might yield, stemming from sources like market volatility, economic downturns or factors specific to individual companies. There's always a chance that you could lose a portion or even all of your invested money. The degree of risk tied to an investment directly correlates with the asset class and specific securities you choose.

The reward, or return, on an investment is the profit you earn over and above your initial investment. This profit may come as capital gains (price appreciation of your investments) or income, such as interest or dividends. High-reward investments are generally sought after, but it's crucial to acknowledge the elevated risk that accompanies them. Each investor has a unique risk tolerance, influenced by variables like their financial objectives, investment timeline and personal comfort level with uncertainty. Those with high risk tolerance may be comfortable investing in volatile assets for a shot at greater returns, while those with low risk tolerance might favor more stable investments, even if it implies potentially lower returns.

Active versus passive investing

The domain of investment is often categorized into two overarching strategies: active and passive investing. The choice between the two hinges on several factors, including financial objectives, risk tolerance, level of investment knowledge and the time one can devote. Active investing necessitates active engagement, wherein the investor or their appointed portfolio manager routinely engages in buying and selling investments with the objective of surpassing the market or a specific benchmark. This approach is based on the premise that it's possible to exploit market inefficiencies through in-depth analysis and experience.

On the contrary, passive investing is a long haul strategy that involves purchasing and retaining a diversified portfolio of assets with the goal of emulating market performance over time. This strategy is typically executed through vehicles like index funds or ETFs that reflect the constitution of a market index. For most individual investors, a passive strategy proves more suitable, as it involves fewer transactions (thus, lower transaction costs), less stress and usually yields better long-term results.

Stocks

Equity or stock market investment is a prevalent strategy for wealth creation and rightly so. Stocks, also known as shares of a company, signify an ownership fraction in that corporation. When you buy a stock, you're essentially acquiring a minor share in that company, making you a shareholder. One of the main reasons investors gravitate toward stocks is their high-growth potential. As a company flourishes, its profits escalate, leading to a consequent rise in its stock value. This growth can yield significant returns for the investors. For example, if you bought a company share at $50 and the value surges to $100, you've effectively doubled your initial investment. Some companies also distribute a part of their profits back to their shareholders in the form of dividends. These payments are usually made regularly, often on a quarterly basis, and offer a continuous income stream to shareholders, in addition to any capital appreciation.

While stocks offer the possibility of considerable returns, they also carry a higher degree of risk compared to other investment choices like bonds or savings accounts. Stock values can experience drastic fluctuations within a short span, influenced by numerous factors, including company performance, overall economic conditions and investor sentiment. For example, a company might report earnings below expectations, decide to reduce its dividend or suffer the adverse effects of an economic downturn, all of which could result in a drop in the stock's price. Given the inherent volatility of stocks, diversification proves a critical strategy to mitigate risk. Instead of investing all your funds in a single company's stocks, you can distribute your investments across a variety of companies, sectors and even countries. This way, the poor performance of one stock can be counterbalanced by the performance of others.

Bonds

Bonds function quite differently compared to stocks. When you acquire a bond, you're essentially providing a loan to an entity; this can be a government, a city or a corporation. In return for your loan, the issuer of the bond commits to pay you interest at regular intervals and reimburse the principal amount of the loan at the conclusion of a predetermined term. A primary reason investors incorporate bonds into their portfolios is the regularity of income they present. Bonds yield periodic interest payments, usually bi-annually—an appealing attribute for investors seeking consistent income. The interest rate, often referred to as the coupon rate, is set at the time of issuance, making bond income reliable and steady.

The flip side of bonds' safety and predictability is typically lower potential returns compared to stocks. Although a bond's regular interest payments can provide stable income, they lack the high growth potential that stocks offer. However, this doesn't indicate that bonds can't yield profitable returns. Bond prices can vary in the secondary market based on interest rate alterations. If interest rates decrease, existing bonds with higher coupon rates usually appreciate in value. Similar to stocks, bonds also offer diversification advantages. Because bonds frequently respond differently to market conditions than stocks, owning both in your portfolio can decrease overall risk. When stock prices dip, bond values may remain steady or even rise, counterbalancing losses in your portfolio's stock segment.

There are several types of bonds, each with different risk and return properties. Government bonds, such as U.S. treasuries, are deemed among the safest investments because they're supported by the full faith and credit of the U.S. government. Corporate bonds, issued by companies, generally offer higher returns to offset the increased risk. Municipal bonds, issued by states, cities or other local bodies, are beneficial as they're exempt from federal taxes and sometimes state and local taxes as well.

Mutual funds

Mutual funds provide investors with an opportunity to invest in a diversified portfolio of assets without the need to purchase each security individually. They can be an efficient and uncomplicated way for investors, particularly those new to investing or with limited resources, to achieve diversification. Like all investments, they have their unique traits and costs. The main allure of a mutual fund is the capacity to invest in a wide array of assets, offering instant diversification. This diversification can minimize investment risk by distributing the funds across various investments. Some mutual funds hold hundreds or even thousands of different stocks or bonds, which means the downfall of any single investment will have a smaller impact on the overall portfolio.

Alongside diversification, mutual funds also offer accessibility. With a comparatively small investment, investors can own a portion of a portfolio that comprises a wide mix of investments. Achieving this level of diversification would be challenging with a small amount of capital if purchasing individual securities. Mutual funds are managed by professional portfolio managers. These experts research, choose and track the performance of the securities purchased by the fund. For investors who lack the time or expertise to manage their portfolios, this professional management can be a significant advantage.

One of the crucial considerations when investing in mutual funds is the cost. Mutual funds carry management fees, known as expense ratios, which cover the management costs of the fund, including the compensation of the fund's managers. The expense ratio is articulated as a percentage of the fund's assets each year. Apart from the expense ratio, some mutual funds also impose a sales commission, also known as a load. Load funds charge a percentage of your investment either at the time of purchase (front-end load) or when you sell your shares (back-end load).

There are numerous types of mutual funds, each to fulfill a specific investment objective. Some mutual funds concentrate on stocks, others on bonds, and some blend the two. There are also sector-specific funds, international funds, index funds and target-date funds, among others.

ETFs

Like mutual funds, ETFs provide an opportunity to invest in a diversified portfolio of assets. An ETF might trace a specific index such as the S&P 500, a sector of the economy or a distinctive investment style. This wide-ranging exposure can assist in risk reduction and eliminates the necessity to choose individual stocks or bonds. A key advantage ETFs possess over mutual funds is their tradability.

While mutual funds are priced once at the closure of each trading day, ETFs are traded on exchanges in the same way as individual stocks. This means you can purchase and sell ETFs throughout the trading day, providing greater flexibility. ETFs are typically passively managed, which means their goal is to match the performance of a specific index rather than surpass it. This strategy decreases the amount of buying and selling the fund needs to do, consequently reducing transaction costs. As a result, ETFs generally have lower expense ratios than actively managed mutual funds.

Another substantial benefit of ETFs is their transparency. Most ETFs reveal their holdings daily, unlike traditional mutual funds, which disclose their holdings quarterly. This transparency enables investors to understand exactly what assets they own through their ETF. ETFs also tend to be more tax-efficient than mutual funds due to their structure. This efficiency originates from the "in-kind" creation and redemption process of ETF shares, which can help limit the capital gains distributions on which investors have to pay taxes. ETFs offer the same kind of flexibility that you get when trading stocks. You can purchase ETF shares on margin, short sell shares or hold for the long term. Furthermore, minimum investment requirements for ETFs are typically lower than those for mutual funds, making them a convenient choice for novice investors.

Real estate

Real estate investing involves acquiring, managing, leasing or selling properties for financial gain. The most common type is residential real estate, which consists of properties like houses, apartments and townhouses. Commercial real estate, which includes office spaces, shopping malls and industrial properties, is another significant category.

Various strategies can be applied when investing in real estate. These include the buy-and-hold strategy, in which an investor buys a property and rents it out for ongoing income; flipping, for which an investor purchases a property, upgrades it and sells it for a profit; and real estate investment trusts (REITs), offering investors a chance to invest in large-scale, income-generating real estate. Real estate can offer continuous income (cash flow) if the property is rented out for more than its associated expenses. Furthermore, properties can appreciate over time, potentially offering a profit upon sale. In some regions, tax benefits related to real estate investment are available, including deductions for mortgage interest, property taxes and operational expenses. Depreciation deductions might also be possible.

Real estate investing enables the use of leverage, the capacity to utilize borrowed funds, to increase the potential return on investment. By getting a mortgage, you can buy a pricier property than you could otherwise afford, potentially enhancing your return if the property appreciates. Although real estate can offer attractive returns, it carries certain risks. These include market volatility, vacancies, property damage and liquidity risk (the ease with which an asset can be bought or sold). Investing in real estate will not be a part of the investment strategy I recommend, but you should be aware of the option.

Cryptocurrency

Cryptocurrencies have emerged as a new asset class over the last decade, drawing attention from investors worldwide for their potential for high returns, albeit paired with substantial volatility. Cryptocurrencies are digital or virtual currencies that employ cryptography for security and function on decentralized platforms called blockchain technology. Bitcoin is the most famous cryptocurrency, but there are thousands of others, often referred to as altcoins (alternative coins), including Ethereum, Ripple and Litecoin, among others.

The primary reason many investors are drawn to cryptocurrencies is the extraordinary returns some have experienced. For example, Bitcoin, introduced in 2009, traded for pennies for a time and has reached valuations of tens of thousands of dollars per coin. This striking increase in value has generated significant wealth for some investors, triggering widespread interest. Cryptocurrencies are noted for their extreme volatility. Prices can shift drastically in a brief period, making it possible for investors to experience major gains or losses. This volatility can present opportunities, but it also heightens the risk.

As a novel and rapidly developing space, the regulatory environment surrounding cryptocurrencies is uncertain and can significantly impact their value. Different countries have varied regulations concerning their use, trading and taxation. Some countries welcome them, while others have entirely banned them. Cryptocurrencies are stored in digital wallets, which can be susceptible to hacking. Several notable cryptocurrency exchanges have been hacked, leading to significant losses for investors. If you choose to invest, prioritizing security, using trusted exchanges and considering storing your cryptocurrency in a secure wallet are crucial. While some believe they represent the future of money and finance, others view them as a speculative bubble. The truth likely lies somewhere in between.

If you want to invest in cryptocurrencies, use Coinbase. Bitcoin and Ethereum are the only two that you need to put money into, you can safely ignore everything else. The vast majority of cryptocurrencies will go to zero and you should not gamble on any of them hoping to strike it rich unless you have expertise and specific domain knowledge of the field. Unlike the S&P 500, there is no reliable basket of cryptocurrencies you can easily purchase. For most people, the best and easiest way to get exposure to crypto is to simply allocate whatever amount of your net worth you are willing to lose in a fifty-fifty split between Bitcoin and Ethereum.

Best Investment

Navigating the sea of investment choices can seem daunting, but I'm here to simplify this journey for you. There's one key investment that you need to comprehend to achieve your early retirement aspirations. This investment stands out for its simplicity, cost effectiveness and consistent track record of robust returns: the S&P 500, particularly through the Vanguard S&P 500 ETF ($VOO).

The S&P 500, short for Standard & Poor's 500, is a key stock market index that tracks the stock performance of 500 of the biggest publicly traded corporations in the United States. It includes a wide variety of businesses across different sectors, thereby serving as a representative snapshot of the U.S. stock market and, by extension, the U.S. economy. Constituents of the S&P 500 are weighted according to their market capitalization, ensuring that the influence of larger companies is proportionally represented in the index. Often, when people discuss how "the market" is performing, they are referencing the S&P 500 due to its comprehensive portrayal of the U.S. corporate landscape and its reflection of the risk/return characteristics of large-cap stocks. The S&P 500 is often described as self-cleansing because it automatically adjusts to reflect the most valuable companies in the U.S. economy. The companies included in the index are not fixed; they're reviewed quarterly and can be replaced based on their market capitalization, liquidity, domicile, public float, sector classification, financial viability and length of time publicly traded on an exchange. This means that the S&P 500 inherently drops companies that underperform and includes those that show growth potential, ensuring the index stays relevant and reflective of the current economic climate. The S&P 500 spans multiple sectors, including technology, health care, finance, consumer discretionary and more. This broad exposure to different sectors provides a level of diversification within the U.S. equities market, reducing the risk associated with investing in a single sector.

Evaluating the historical performance of an investment is crucial to understanding its potential future behavior under different market conditions. The S&P 500 has demonstrated a reliable and steady pattern of returns throughout its history, making it an attractive proposition for long-term investors. Since its launch in 1926, it has delivered an average annual return of around 10%, assuming dividends are reinvested. Despite occasional periods of volatility and market downturns, the index has consistently exhibited an upward trend over the long term. This robust performance can be attributed to the S&P 500's composition, which primarily consists of large, established companies that are frequently industry leaders. These firms have proven their ability to generate steady profits and often, regular dividend payments. Even if you had invested at the peak before the 2008 market crash, you would still have seen considerable growth in your investment if you had remained invested and continually reinvested your dividends.

The Vanguard S&P 500 ETF, or $VOO, is a fund designed to mimic the performance of the S&P 500 by holding the same stocks in equivalent proportions. Managed by Vanguard, renowned as one of the world's largest investment firms for its cost-efficient offerings, $VOO is a favored choice among investors seeking to parallel the performance of the S&P 500 for many reasons.

To maximize returns, it's crucial to curb costs wherever feasible. Each dollar spent on fees is a dollar less of potential earnings. $VOO is often highlighted for its cost-efficient structure, making it a prime choice for expense-aware investors. An expense ratio, which is the annual fee that funds or ETFs charge their shareholders, is a representation of the percentage of the fund's total assets used for operational expenses. These fees cover a variety of costs such as fund management, legal services, administrative expenses and record keeping. $VOO is known for its remarkably low expense ratio, often less than 0.05%. This is substantially lower than many other mutual funds and ETFs, some of which have expense ratios exceeding 1%. Although the difference in expense ratios may seem negligible in terms of percentages, its long-term impact can be considerable, thanks to the power of compounding. For instance, suppose you invest $10,000 and it grows at 7% per year for 30 years. Without any costs, it would amount to nearly $76,123. Now, consider a 1% expense ratio, the final sum after 30 years drops to $57,435, a difference of almost $20,000. With an expense ratio as low as $VOO's 0.05%, the final sum would be $74,872, much closer to the sum without any costs.

Irrespective of your investment know-how or financial standing, $VOO makes investing in a diverse array of stocks not just achievable, but fairly straightforward. $VOO can be purchased on most major investment platforms and can be traded like individual stocks during regular market hours, giving investors a greater degree of flexibility and control. Whether you're employing a traditional brokerage account, an online trading platform or a robo-advisor, it's highly likely that $VOO will be listed among the investment options. Unlike some mutual funds, which demand a substantial minimum investment, $VOO, being an ETF, has no such prerequisites. You can initiate your investment journey by buying just one share. This absence of a minimum investment threshold renders $VOO an attractive choice for novice investors or those with limited investment capital. It facilitates incremental investing, a method of regularly investing small amounts, which is an effective strategy for steadily building wealth over time.

The user friendliness and lack of a minimum investment requirement for $VOO opens the door for implementing dollar-cost averaging (DCA). DCA is an investment tactic that involves investing a fixed sum in the same fund or security at regular intervals, regardless of its price. Over time, DCA can help soften the impact of market volatility and lower the risk of making a significant investment just before a market downturn. Given its accessibility on most investment platforms and the absence of a minimum investment requirement, $VOO presents itself as a convenient and flexible choice for both beginner and seasoned investors. Whether you're planning a one-off investment or aiming to invest consistently over time, $VOO emerges as an attractive and easy option to gain broad market exposure.

Another benefit is the feature to automatically reinvest dividends. While this may appear a minor detail initially, it's actually an incredibly potent strategy that can substantially amplify the growth potential of your investment. Dividends are a part of a company's earnings that are shared with shareholders, generally as a means to redistribute surplus profits back to the investors. When you hold shares of an ETF like $VOO, which includes 500 of the largest U.S. companies, you essentially own a tiny piece of these businesses and, therefore, are eligible to receive a share of their disbursed profits. $VOO provides the choice for investors to automatically reinvest these dividends back into the fund, in turn buying more shares. This strategy, known as "dividend reinvestment," serves as a critical catalyst for compounding, which refers to an exponential rise in investment value over time. By reinvesting dividends, you're not only earning a return on your initial investment but also on the returns that have been reinvested. The reinvested dividends will generate their own dividends and if these are reinvested, too, they will also produce dividends, creating a compounding cycle. This can significantly bolster your total return over the long haul. Dividend reinvestment can be likened to a snowball rolling downhill. As it rolls, it gathers more snow, growing larger and gaining speed. Similarly, when you reinvest dividends, your portfolio swells over time and as it expands, it yields more dividends, which can then be reinvested.

Numerous respected financial experts and accomplished investors have publicly advocated for the strategy of investing in S&P 500 index funds such as $VOO. One such advocate is Warren Buffett, widely regarded as one of the most successful investors globally. His steadfast endorsement of low-cost index funds stems from a place of deep knowledge and experience. Recognized for his value investing strategy and astute business wisdom, Buffett's advice holds considerable clout in the investment world. His support for S&P 500 index funds, and by extension $VOO, hinges on their sustained performance, affordability and accessibility for the average investor. Buffett famously instructed the trustee of his estate to invest 90% of his wealth into an S&P 500 index fund for his wife after his demise, a ringing endorsement of his confidence in the strategy.

In 2007, Warren Buffett proposed a now-famous bet that a passive investment in an S&P 500 index fund would outperform a meticulously curated portfolio of hedge funds over a decade. He staked $1 million on his claim, arguing that the exorbitant fees associated with active management often do not yield better investment outcomes for investors. Protégé Partners LLC, an asset management firm, accepted Buffett's challenge and selected five funds-of-funds, the identities of which were not disclosed. Fast forward to the close of 2017, a decade later, Buffett's chosen S&P 500 index fund (invested in Vanguard's Admiral Shares, an S&P 500 index fund) considerably outpaced Protégé Partners' hedge fund portfolio. The S&P 500 index fund delivered an average annual return of 8.5%, whereas the hedge fund portfolio only managed an average annual return of roughly 3%. The bet's proceeds were donated to charity, but it effectively demonstrated Buffett's unwavering faith in passive investing and spotlighted the difficulty active fund managers face in beating broad market indices, particularly after accounting for fees.

The allure of investing in low-cost index funds for a vast number of investors lies in its straightforwardness and efficacy. Investors aren't required to perform complex analyses, time the market or handpick individual stocks. They can rely on the index fund's inherent diversification and passive nature to generate returns that have consistently outperformed a majority of actively managed funds in the long run. A study by S&P Dow Jones Indices found that over the decade ending December 2020, 88% of large cap fund managers fell short of outperforming the S&P 500. Moreover, a majority of active managers in most categories underperformed their benchmarks even over shorter periods. Fees also play a pivotal role. Many hedge funds adopt the "2 and 20" fee structure, which involves charging a 2% management fee and then claiming 20% of any profits; a pricey fee to pay just to underperform the S&P.

When people advise investing in the market, they're generally referring to the S&P 500. If $VOO is unavailable in your country, I recommend finding the most similar ETF available with the lowest expense ratios.

Bonds and Portfolio Allocation

Investing in bonds is an important part of a balanced investment portfolio for several reasons. Bonds can provide a counterbalance to the more volatile nature of stocks. When stock markets are not performing well, bonds tend to hold their value better and this can stabilize your portfolio during market downturns. This can make them an attractive option for investors who prefer a lower-risk investment or are nearing retirement and want to protect their portfolio from large swings in value. Bonds pay interest, providing a predictable stream of income. This can be particularly attractive to retirees or other investors who need to generate a certain level of income from their investment portfolios.

The Vanguard Total Bond Market ETF ($BND) serves as a comprehensive representation of the U.S. bond market. This ETF provides investors with extensive diversification by allocating funds across a vast range of public, investment-grade, taxable and fixed income securities. In its pursuit to mirror the Bloomberg Barclays U.S. Aggregate Float Adjusted Index's performance, $BND comprises a diverse blend of government bonds, corporate bonds and international dollar–denominated bonds.

Government bonds, a key component of $BND, are bonds that the U.S. federal government issues. They are frequently regarded as the safest form of bond investment due to the "full faith and credit" backing by the U.S. government. This category includes Treasury bonds, notes and bills; financial instruments with virtually zero default risk because the government guarantees them. Corporate bonds, another important ingredient in $BND's portfolio, are bonds that private companies issue to raise capital for various purposes like business expansion, research and development or debt refinancing. Compared to government bonds, corporate bonds usually offer a higher yield to compensate for the increased risk associated with them. The probability of repayment is intrinsically linked to the financial stability and profitability of the company that issues them. International Dollar–Denominated Bonds make up the last component of $BND. These bonds are issued by foreign entities but are denominated in U.S. dollars. This type of bond allows investors to gain exposure to overseas entities while insulating them from the inherent risks associated with foreign currency fluctuations.

The diversified nature of the $BND offers a safeguard against the volatility associated with individual bonds. It can therefore be an effective choice for investors seeking a consistent income source and a balanced level of risk. Additionally, its low expense ratio presents a cost-efficient method for investors to tap into the extensive U.S. bond market. Like most bond funds, $BND pays out regular income in the form of monthly dividends from the interest payments on its bonds. This can make it an attractive choice for income-focused investors. $BND is managed by experts who adjust the holdings as needed to align with the index that the fund tracks. This takes the burden off individual investors who may not have the time or expertise to manage their own bond portfolios.

An investor's asset allocation is arguably one of the most consequential decisions they can make. It has a significant influence on both the risk level and potential return of their investment portfolio. Investors typically vary their asset allocation based on their financial goals, risk tolerance and investment horizon. Here, we explore two different strategies: One prioritizes wealth accumulation (100% Vanguard S&P 500 ETF or $VOO) and the other focuses on wealth preservation (70% $VOO, 25% Vanguard Total Bond Market ETF or $BND, and 5% cash).

The aggressive 100% $VOO strategy is typically best suited to individuals in their wealth-building phase. By investing the entire portfolio in the $VOO, an ETF designed to track the performance of the S&P 500 Index, investors gain exposure to a wide-ranging segment of the U.S. equity market. With 100% allocation in equities, this portfolio aims to maximize potential returns by harnessing the traditionally superior long-term growth of the stock market.

The rationale behind this strategy is rooted in historical data that suggests equities (specifically, the S&P 500) have delivered higher returns over the long term than other asset classes. Although there are periods of downturns and volatility, the overall trend for equities has been upward. That's why for individuals in their wealth-building phase, especially those who can afford to take on higher risk and have the patience to ride out market volatility, this strategy can yield substantial growth.

The balanced 70% $VOO, 25% $BND, 5% cash portfolio strategy comes into play when individuals approach retirement or reach a stage in their lives at which preserving capital takes precedence over aggressive growth. It marks a shift in investment strategy, from a high-risk–high-return model to one that seeks to balance steady growth, income generation and risk mitigation. The allocation of 70% in $VOO allows the portfolio to continue benefiting from the growth potential of equities. While less aggressive than the 100% $VOO strategy, this allocation still provides substantial exposure to the broad U.S. equity market and the potential for capital appreciation that it offers.

The inclusion of 25% in the Vanguard Total Bond Market ETF ($BND) introduces an element of income generation and stability to the portfolio. Bonds, while typically offering lower returns than equities, are considered less volatile. They provide regular income in the form of interest payments and the return of the principal upon maturity is guaranteed if held to term. $BND specifically offers broad exposure to U.S. investment-grade bonds, further diversifying the portfolio across different types of bonds, including U.S. Treasuries, corporate bonds and mortgage-backed securities. This income and stability component of the portfolio can help buffer against stock market volatility, thereby reducing the portfolio's overall risk.

Finally, maintaining 5% of the portfolio in cash provides further safety and flexibility. Having cash on hand allows investors to take advantage of new investment opportunities as they arise without needing to sell existing investments. It also acts as a buffer, providing immediate funds to cover unexpected expenses or losses, without the need to withdraw from potentially underperforming investments.

Compounding

Compounding, one of the most powerful principles in financial management, often goes underappreciated or misunderstood despite being a pillar in the process of wealth creation. This concept, although simple, plays an influential role in growing an investor's wealth over time. To bring this principle to life and highlight its transformative potential, let's explore the illustrative tale of two brothers, Alex and Ben.

Alex and Ben are both 25 years old, recently embarked on their professional journeys. They have their whole lives ahead of them but have already developed an understanding of the significance of saving and investing for the future. They dream of retiring comfortably at the age of 65. However, the way they approach their investing journey varies dramatically.

The Proactive Investor: Alex

Alex decides to hit the ground running and immediately starts investing a portion of his income. He puts $5,000 each year into an S&P 500 index fund, which historically yields an average annual return of about 10%. After ten years of diligent and regular investing, Alex stops contributing further to his fund. Instead, he allows his accumulated investments to sit and compound over the next 30 years.

The Late Bloomer: Ben

On the other hand, Ben chooses to revel in the joys of his youth and holds off on investing until he turns 35. This is the same age when Alex stopped actively contributing to his investment fund. Once Ben starts investing, he mirrors Alex's strategy by allocating $5,000 each year to the same index fund. He continues this pattern for the next 30 years until he reaches the age of 65.

The Reveal

Upon reaching 65, a startling contrast emerges between the brothers' investment outcomes. Alex, who only invested a total of $50,000, finds his portfolio has grown to an impressive $1.39

million. This dramatic growth, propelled over the three decades it was left untouched, was fueled by the remarkable power of compounding.

Contrarily, Ben, despite contributing $150,000, a sum three times larger than Alex's initial investment, accumulates approximately $820,000. This is a substantial amount but pales in comparison to Alex's returns. Despite his longer investment timeline, three times that of Alex's, Ben's final portfolio value is less than his brother's.

This striking divergence in Alex and Ben's financial outcomes can be attributed to the potency of compound interest. What set Alex's trajectory apart was the advantage of time. Although he contributed less capital, his early entry into investing allowed his returns ample opportunity to generate their own earnings. This self-perpetuating cycle of earning interest on interest results in the exponential growth of an investment.

Alex and Ben's story paints a vivid picture of the transformative power of early and consistent saving and investing. It drives home the vital lesson that timing plays a significant role in the journey toward wealth creation. The earlier you begin investing, the more time you give your money to benefit from the miraculous influence of compounding. Therefore, regardless of the initial amount, it's essential to embark on your investment journey at the earliest opportunity. Even modest amounts can grow significantly over time, thanks to the extraordinary power of compounding. Let's look at what would happen if you invested every single year and let the money compound until you are 65, based on when you start:

Starting Age	Years Until 65	$2,000/Year Contribution	$5,000/Year Contribution	$10,000/Year Contribution
45	20	$114,091.80	$285,916.80	$572,520.89
40	25	$195,907.34	$490,948.52	$983,077.21
35	30	$327,672.09	$821,154.16	$1,644,282.25
30	35	$539,880.54	$1,352,953.65	$2,709,159.59
25	40	$881,644.37	$2,209,422.04	$4,424,155.19
20	45	$1,432,058.44	$3,588,772.95	$7,186,172.75

In the grand scheme of things, it's not just about how much you save and invest, but when you start. The tale of two brothers and our compound interest table serves as a reminder of this invaluable truth in the world of investing and personal finance.

Investing Styles

Coming into a significant sum of money, whether through an inheritance, a hefty bonus or a successful business sale, can raise a host of questions about how best to manage and invest. Two of the primary strategies people often consider are lump sum investing, in which you invest all the money at once, and DCA, where you distribute the investment over a certain period.

DCA

This investment strategy involves systematically spreading out the total investment amount over a predefined period, irrespective of market conditions. This approach aims to reduce the risk associated with making a large investment in a volatile market and thereby insulate against short-term fluctuations in the asset's price. In essence, it strips away the complexities of trying to time the market to purchase equities at the most favorable prices. Moreover, DCA provides a structured and automated way to consistently contribute to your investments, often via monthly increments.

For instance, if you decide to invest in an S&P 500 index fund using DCA, you might invest $1,000 each month for an entire year, regardless of the index fund's price each month. The intention here is to accumulate a sizable position in the fund over time while mitigating the risk of investing a large sum at a less than optimal moment. As we mentioned before, you can automate this process, thus taking away the manual burden of transferring money from your bank every paycheck.

Lump sum investing

On the other hand, lump sum investing involves investing a large sum of money all at once. For instance, if you inherit $50,000 and decide to invest all of it in an S&P 500 index fund at once, you're utilizing a lump sum investing approach.

Which strategy triumphs?

The financial community has extensively debated the merits and demerits of both strategies, sparking a heated conversation about which one typically garners superior results. Research has often favored lump sum investing in a theoretical sense. According to a study conducted by Vanguard, lump sum investing outperformed DCA approximately 66% of the time over rolling 12-month periods between 1926 and 2011. The logic behind this outcome lies in the historical trend of markets generally appreciating over time. Therefore, the sooner you can expose your money to the market, the more opportunity it has to grow.

While studies might suggest a statistical advantage for lump sum investing, it's important not to discount the advantages of DCA, which has distinct attributes that might make it a more fitting choice for some investors. One of the key benefits of DCA is that it inherently serves as a risk mitigation strategy. By distributing your investments over time, you guard against the risk of allocating all your funds at a market peak. If you invest a large sum in one go and the market takes a downturn shortly after, your portfolio could suffer significant losses.

Conversely, DCA, with its incremental investments, allows you to navigate the ups and downs of the market in a more controlled way. From a psychological standpoint, DCA can be a more manageable approach for many investors. The prospect of investing a sizable amount all at once can be quite daunting, especially for those new to the investment world. If the market plunges soon after such a large investment, it could be tremendously demoralizing and might shake an investor's confidence. However, by utilizing DCA, you spread your investments over time, smoothing out your exposure to market volatility. This strategy reduces the likelihood of encountering a significant decline immediately after investing and can bring peace of mind.

Ultimately, the choice between DCA and lump sum investing hinges on individual factors. If you suddenly find yourself with a substantial sum to invest, take time to reflect on your personal risk tolerance, financial objectives and psychological comfort level with different investment approaches. You might also consider combining the two strategies in a way that suits your circumstances. For example, you could invest a portion of your money as a lump sum and then use DCA for the remaining amount. Remember, the essential part of investing isn't necessarily the exact method you employ, but rather the act of investing itself. Consistently setting money aside for the future and allowing it to grow over time is a crucial aspect of financial planning, regardless of whether you choose DCA, lump sum investing or a blend of both.

Financial Advisors

In our modern, tech-driven era, a plethora of services promising to simplify your investing journey exist, ranging from robo-advisors and investment apps to traditional human advisors. Deciding which of these services best suits your needs can be a daunting task. Here, we're going to discuss the potential drawbacks of these services and why they might not always live up to the hype.

Robo-advisors are digital platforms offering automated financial planning services steered by sophisticated algorithms, with little to no human intervention. They gather information about your financial situation and goals via online questionnaires and use this data to provide advice and automatically manage your investments. The attraction of robo-advisors lies in their user-friendly interfaces and easy accessibility. They handle tasks like portfolio creation and rebalancing and because their operations are automated, they can provide these services at a lower cost compared to traditional advisors. However, it's crucial to note that while robo-advisors can be a valuable tool for beginner investors or those managing smaller portfolios, they frequently underperform the S&P 500. Consequently, you might find yourself paying a fee for a service that doesn't even match the performance of a low-cost S&P 500 index fund like $VOO, which you could easily manage on your own.

On the other hand, investment advisors or financial advisors are professionals who offer investment advice or comprehensive financial planning services. Compared to robo-advisors, these professionals can offer a broader range of services, including but not limited to, retirement planning, tax planning and investment advice. While an investment advisor can provide personalized advice that a robo-advisor can't, there are potential drawbacks to consider. First, they are typically more expensive. Advisors generally charge a fee based on a percentage of assets managed, which can considerably erode your returns over the long term. Second, the quality of advice can vary widely among advisors. Some may prioritize their own interests over yours, recommending investments that earn them higher commissions instead of those that best fit your financial objectives. While the world of financial advisory services can seem attractive at first glance, it's essential to approach them with a critical eye. Consider the cost, the value they provide and how they align with your financial goals and investment strategy. Often, taking charge of your own investments, starting with a straightforward index fund like $VOO, could be a more cost-effective and rewarding approach.

The essence of the S&P 500 index investing approach lies in its simplicity and consistency. If you maintain discipline, exhibit patience and stick to this uncomplicated investment strategy, you can sidestep the need for services like robo-advisors or investment advisors. Through regular investment in a broad-based index fund such as $VOO, you're effectively reflecting the performance of the overall market. Simultaneously, you avoid the advisory fees that, although may seem small at first, could significantly eat into your returns over an extended period. For most people aiming to accumulate wealth over the long term, a straightforward, consistent investment in the S&P 500 is sufficient. One of the golden rules of investing is to minimize costs and self-managing your investments is a practical way to adhere to this principle.

In the end, investing should be viewed as a marathon, not a sprint. It's about creating sustainable wealth over time. By staying committed to a simple and consistent strategy, understanding your risk tolerance and avoiding unnecessary fees, you are more likely to achieve your long-term financial goals. Remember, investing is not just about making money but also about preserving and growing it for the future. Simplicity is the key to unlocking this potential.

The Power of Habit

Habits are the threads that weave together to create the fabric of our daily existence. Often operating beneath our conscious awareness, these automated behaviors govern the majority of our actions, from the mundane, such as our morning routines, to the significant, including our spending and saving patterns. While habits are often discussed in the context of health or productivity, their importance extends far deeper into our lives, most notably influencing our financial well-being. Money habits, the decisions and actions we routinely make concerning our finances, play a crucial role in shaping our current financial status and the trajectory of our financial future. Just as a healthy eating habit can determine our physical wellness, financial habits can dictate our economic health. They influence how we earn, spend, save and invest, shaping our financial landscape.

At the heart of every habit lies a simple yet powerful structure known as the "habit loop." This model, composed of three integral components—cue, routine and reward—provides a valuable framework to understand how habits are formed and how they function.

A cue is a trigger that initiates the habit. It could be a specific time of day, an emotional state, a location or even the company of certain people. Let's illustrate this with a habit geared toward investing. In the context of personal finance, the cue could be receiving your paycheck. The routine is the behavior itself—the action we automatically engage in following the cue. The routine might be immediately transferring a certain percentage of your earnings to a savings or investment account. Finally, the reward is the positive reinforcement that follows the routine. It provides the motivation to repeat the behavior in the future. The reward could be the satisfaction of seeing your savings grow and getting closer to your financial goals.

To create habits that lead to wealth accumulation and early retirement, the first step is identifying cues that can trigger beneficial financial behaviors. These cues should be consistent and frequent enough to encourage regular engagement with the routine. For example, the arrival of a paycheck, a daily calendar reminder or even a simple sticky note on your computer could act as cues.

Next, the routine should be a specific financial action that contributes to wealth building. This could be anything from investing a certain amount in a retirement account, to tracking daily expenses, reviewing and optimizing your budget or spending time learning about personal finance. The key is to start small and gradually increase the complexity or intensity of the routine as the habit solidifies.

Finally, the reward should provide immediate satisfaction, encouraging the repetition of the routine. This could be as simple as the gratification from knowing you're making progress toward your financial goals or more tangible rewards like treating yourself to a favorite activity or experience.

Understanding the habit loop also plays a critical role in breaking unhealthy financial habits that may be hindering your wealth accumulation. By identifying the cues and rewards that drive these behaviors, you can begin to restructure or eliminate these habits. For example, if you find that stress (cue) leads you to engage in retail therapy (routine) and you feel temporary relief afterward (reward), finding alternative stress-management techniques can help break this cycle. For example, upon identifying stress as a trigger, you might opt for meditation, exercise or engaging in a hobby. These activities can serve as new routines, providing stress relief (the desired reward) without the negative financial implications of shopping.

Building wealth and achieving early retirement isn't about making a few large financial decisions; it's about consistently making many small, beneficial decisions. And habits are the most effective tool to ensure this consistency. Understanding the habit loop is vital, as it not only provides insights into why we do what we do but also equips us with the knowledge to alter our behaviors, if needed. Once we know what triggers our habits (cue), what we do (routine) and why we do it (reward), we gain the power to intentionally craft our financial habits to serve our long-term goals. Whether it's starting a new habit of saving a certain amount each month or breaking an old habit of impulsive spending, understanding the habit loop can be a game changer in our journey toward financial independence.

Chapter 8

BEYOND
THE HORIZON

It's time to explore the important considerations that come into play after you've achieved F.I.R.E. Just as you needed a strategy to reach F.I.R.E., you will need one to maintain it as well. From managing the risks of market fluctuations, to ensuring your health care needs are met, to adjusting your spending strategies to maximize your retirement savings, there are numerous aspects to think about in your post-F.I.R.E. life. We will also discuss the psychological aspects of this transition, from finding fulfillment in your newfound freedom to managing the emotional challenges that come with such a drastic lifestyle shift.

The Pursuit of Happiness

How does one ensure that their years of financial independence are not only prosperous but also fulfilled and content? The answer lies in understanding the science of well-being. Before delving into the science, it's important to define well-being. It's not merely the absence of negative emotions but the presence of positive ones. It's the profound satisfaction with life, a sense of purpose and the ability to manage stress effectively. It's the harmony of the mind, body and spirit. Ultimately, well-being is about cultivating a high quality of life. The concept of well-being is more than just a state of health or happiness; it is the holistic sense of living a fulfilling, meaningful and content life. Psychologist Martin Seligman, a pioneer in the field of positive psychology, proposed the PERMA model to outline the five essential elements that contribute to human well-being: positive emotion, engagement, relationships, meaning and accomplishment.

The first pillar, positive emotion, extends far beyond the simplistic concept of happiness. It encapsulates a rich range of emotions—joy, gratitude, serenity, interest, hope, pride, amusement, inspiration, awe and love—that nourish the soul, elevate the spirit and enhance life experiences. The cultivation of these emotions can create an undercurrent of positivity that bolsters resilience, broadens perspective and fuels personal growth, especially significant in the context of retirement. Joy springs from moments of delight, success or good fortune. It's a spontaneous and often contagious emotion that can be magnified by sharing. In retirement, one might derive joy from spending time with loved ones, discovering new hobbies or simply appreciating the freedom and leisure time that retirement offers.

Gratitude is the emotion we feel in response to receiving a benefit, gift or act of kindness. A regular gratitude practice, such as maintaining a gratitude journal or expressing thanks to others, can help shift our focus from what's missing or wrong to what's going well in our lives, fostering a sense of contentment and fulfillment. Serenity, or inner peace, arises when we are in a state of calm contentment. It often requires living in the present moment and accepting things as they are, instead of constantly yearning for more or fretting about the past or future. Regular mindfulness or meditation practice can cultivate serenity and balance in our lives. Interest ignites our curiosity and propels us to explore and learn.

Whether it's delving into a new book, picking up a new hobby or traveling to a new destination, nurturing our interests keeps the mind active and engaged. Hope is the optimistic emotion we feel about a better future. Even amidst challenges and uncertainties, maintaining hope can be empowering and motivating. Setting meaningful goals and planning actionable steps toward them can help foster hope in retirement. Pride emerges when we acknowledge our achievements and successes. Taking time to celebrate our accomplishments, big or small, can build confidence and self-esteem.

Amusement arises from situations that are funny or entertaining. A good sense of humor not only lightens mood but also strengthens social connections. Inspiration motivates us to strive for our goals and aspirations. It often stems from witnessing human virtues or achievements or immersing ourselves in nature's beauty. Awe is the emotion we experience in the presence of something grand or profound that transcends our understanding of the world. Encountering awe-inspiring experiences can significantly boost our well-being. Love, the most profound of all emotions, encompasses a deep affection, attachment or care for someone or something. Investing time and energy in nurturing our relationships can fill our retirement years with love, warmth and connection.

While positive emotions often arise naturally, they can also be consciously cultivated. Engaging in activities that spark joy, practicing mindfulness, nurturing relationships, pursuing hobbies and maintaining an optimistic outlook on life can foster these emotions.

The second pillar, engagement, emphasizes the significance of immersing oneself completely in activities that are not only interesting, but also challenging and inspiring. Intense focus and absorption are often referred to as a "flow" state, a concept developed by psychologist Mihaly Csikszentmihalyi. Flow is a state of effortless concentration so deep that we lose our sense of time, ourselves and our problems, and are completely and fully "in the moment." This is akin to the runner's high, the writer's trance or the climber's exhilaration amidst the gravity-defying ascent, moments of rapt immersion that people report as some of the most enjoyable of their lives.

When we are engaged in an activity that we love, we are more likely to experience positive emotions, exhibit greater creativity and even find more satisfaction in the work we do. Moreover, the experience of flow can also help reduce anxiety, boost mood and improve overall sense of well-being. In the context of retirement, engagement takes on a crucial role. Without the demands of work, retirees often find they have a vast amount of time to fill. Engagement in meaningful activities can provide structure, purpose and fulfillment, turning the golden years into a period of personal growth and exploration.

Identifying activities that lead to a flow state can vary wildly from person to person and it often requires some introspection and experimentation. One person might find flow in the serene precision of painting, while another might find it in the rhythmic agility required in playing an instrument. For some, it might be the invigorating challenge of hiking up a mountain trail, while for others, it could be the quiet satisfaction of crafting a compelling story or the exhilaration of engaging in a captivating conversation.

The key to engagement is identifying those activities that deeply resonate and provide a sense of satisfaction and fulfillment. This could be a hobby that was set aside during the busy years of career building and family raising or it could be a new interest that has only recently sparked curiosity. No matter the activity, the purpose remains the same: to immerse oneself completely, experience the profound state of flow and reap the immense benefits that come with that focus and concentration.

The third pillar, relationships, acknowledges the fundamental human need for connection, companionship and meaningful social interactions. As humans, we are intrinsically social creatures who thrive on the intimacy, support and sense of belonging that positive relationships provide. A substantial body of research underscores the significance of strong, supportive relationships for our mental, emotional and even physical well-being. Relationships offer us a platform for emotional expression, provide us with a sense of identity and present us opportunities to give and receive support. The warmth of companionship, the comfort of a listening ear, the joy of shared laughter—these are just some of the multitude of ways relationships contribute to our overall sense of happiness and fulfillment.

In the context of retirement, the importance of relationships takes on an even greater significance. As work-related obligations recede, we are left with an abundance of time, time that can be invested in nurturing existing relationships and forging new ones. Retirement presents an opportunity to deepen our bonds with our loved ones, to spend quality time with our partner, to get to know our grandchildren, to reconnect with old friends or even to mend strained familial ties. At the same time, it also provides an opportunity to expand our social network.

Joining clubs, participating in community events, volunteering for a cause that resonates with you or simply exploring new social activities can all lead to the formation of new friendships and social connections. In addition to fostering individual relationships, retirement also allows for increased engagement with the community. Community involvement, whether through volunteering, participating in social groups or attending community events, not only offers the chance to meet like-minded individuals, but also provides a sense of purpose and fulfillment that comes from being part of a larger social fabric. By investing in these connections, we bolster our own sense of well-being, infusing our years with love, camaraderie and a deep sense of belonging.

The fourth pillar, meaning, addresses the profound human need to perceive our lives as significant, purposeful and valuable. It refers to a deep-seated sense that we belong to and serve something that transcends our individual existence, adding depth and dimension to our personal experiences. Meaning is not a one-size-fits-all concept. It varies significantly from person to person, often shaped by individual beliefs, values, passions and life experiences. For some, meaning may come from contributing to a larger cause that aligns with their values. For others, it might be found in the pursuit of a passion or in the roles they play within their families, communities or other social contexts.

The transition into retirement, while a major milestone, can sometimes disrupt our sense of meaning and purpose. As work-related identities recede, it becomes vital to find other channels through which to derive meaning and maintain a sense of purpose. Finding meaning in retirement could be as simple as dedicating more time to a beloved hobby, such as gardening, painting or writing. Or, it could involve a more structured commitment, such as volunteering for a community service or contributing to a cause that aligns with your values. Retirement can also be an opportunity to learn new skills, cultivate new passions or even launch a new career or business venture.

Embracing lifelong learning is another way to infuse retirement with meaning. By committing to continuously learning and growing, whether through formal education, self-study or experiential learning, you enrich your life with new knowledge, skills and experiences, thereby adding layers of complexity and interest to your personal narrative. By nurturing a sense of purpose and continuously seeking meaning, we imbue our lives with a sense of significance, creating a rich set of experiences that extend beyond the mundane and toward the extraordinary.

The final pillar, accomplishment, is about more than just achieving goals; it is about striving for success, seeking excellence and engaging in the continuous journey of mastery and growth. It encapsulates our intrinsic drive to succeed, to overcome challenges and to see our efforts come to fruition. In the context of retirement, the concept of accomplishment can take on various forms. Many people worry that retiring from a traditional career will equate to an end of accomplishment.

However, this is a misconception. Retirement is not a cessation of achievement; instead, it offers an opportunity to redirect our energies toward new objectives and goals that can bring personal fulfillment. These goals could range from improving physical fitness, learning a new language, mastering a musical instrument or even writing a book. You might choose to dive deeper into a hobby you've always loved or venture into an entirely new field. The key is to establish personal goals that resonate with your interests and values, and that challenge you to grow and evolve.

The journey toward accomplishment is about embracing challenges, persevering in the face of adversity and relishing the sense of achievement that comes with every step forward. Regardless of the nature or magnitude of our goals, it is this process of striving and achieving that fuels our sense of purpose, keeps us motivated and significantly contributes to our overall well-being.

The PERMA model provides a comprehensive framework for understanding and enhancing our overall well-being. Each pillar is interrelated and collectively contributes to our subjective experience of a fulfilled and meaningful life. As you embark on the journey of early retirement, leveraging these five pillars can guide you in crafting a life of contentment, satisfaction and holistic well-being.

Three-Bucket Strategy for Withdrawals

The sequence of returns risk refers to the danger that the timing of withdrawals from a retirement account will negatively impact the overall rate of return available to the investor. In other words, this risk stems from the timing of investment returns and the order in which these returns are realized. When you're accumulating savings, the sequence of returns doesn't significantly impact the value of your portfolio. However, when you start withdrawing funds, especially during the early years of retirement, the sequence becomes crucial.

The sequence of returns risk can significantly impact your retirement savings, particularly if the market is performing poorly when you begin to withdraw funds. If your retirement coincides with a market downturn and you're withdrawing funds, your overall portfolio could be substantially depleted, making it less likely to recover when markets rebound. This is because you're drawing down a higher percentage of your portfolio when your investments are undervalued. Consequently, even if the market recovers, you may have insufficient funds remaining to benefit fully from the upswing, leading to a quicker depletion of your retirement savings than you anticipated.

One strategy is to adopt flexible spending. This refers to the practice of adjusting your annual expenses based on how the market is performing. When market conditions are tough and your portfolio is underperforming, you can choose to live more frugally and limit your withdrawals. This step helps to preserve your portfolio during trying times. On the other hand, during periods of strong market performance, you can increase your spending a little, allowing you to enjoy the fruits of your investments. This strategy offers a balance between preserving your wealth and enjoying your financial freedom.

The three-bucket strategy is another popular approach to managing retirement assets that aims to provide retirees with income while also mitigating the risks associated with sequence of returns. The strategy involves dividing retirement assets into three separate "buckets" to cover different types of expenses.

Bucket One is for short-term expenses and is filled with highly liquid and safe assets, such as cash or money market funds. It's designed to cover one to two years' worth of living expenses in retirement, excluding the income you may receive from Social Security or pensions. This approach helps to provide a financial cushion that can withstand short-term market fluctuations without necessitating the sale of investments during a market downturn.

Bucket Two is meant to fund your lifestyle in the medium term, during the next three to ten years. This bucket may include a mix of bonds and balanced funds. While riskier than the assets in the first bucket, these investments should offer a higher return to replenish the first bucket as it is depleted and keep up with inflation.

Bucket Three is where your riskier, long-term investments live. This might include stocks, real estate or other growth-oriented assets. This bucket is designed for longer-term growth, intended to refill Buckets One and Two over time. Because this money isn't expected to be needed for many years, it can weather short-term market fluctuations.

The three-bucket strategy helps you organize your retirement savings based on when you'll need to access them. By doing this, you can manage your withdrawal rates more efficiently and better weather market volatility. The cash buffer (Bucket One) ensures you have money for immediate needs, reducing the risk of having to sell investments at a loss during market downturns. This strategy provides a systematic approach to transitioning from accumulation to distribution of assets in retirement, helping to mitigate the sequence of returns risk.

Consider the case of a couple, John and Mary, who have just entered retirement with a portfolio of $1 million. They decide to use the three-bucket strategy to manage their retirement funds.

They allocate $50,000 (5% of their total portfolio) to Bucket One to cover their first two years of retirement.

Bucket Two receives $250,000 (25% of their portfolio), which is invested in $BND.

The remainder of their portfolio, $700,000 (70%), is allocated to Bucket Three, which is invested in $VOO.

As they progress through retirement, John and Mary use the funds from Bucket One for their daily expenses. Every year, they assess their portfolio and if their long-term investments in Bucket Three have performed well, they shift some money from Bucket Three to Buckets One and Two. This keeps their short-term and medium-term buckets topped up while allowing their long-term investments to continue growing.

This way, the Three-Bucket Strategy provides John and Mary with a clear plan for managing their retirement assets, allowing them to balance their need for income with their desire for long-term growth.

Tax Considerations

Withdrawals from your investment accounts could potentially push you into a higher tax bracket, leading to a heftier tax bill. Here are some strategies to consider to minimize your tax liabilities during retirement.

Tax-advantaged accounts

A critical component of managing your finances as an early retiree revolves around the astute use of tax-advantaged accounts. These accounts, which include options such as 401(k) plans and IRAs, offer substantial tax benefits to incentivize long-term savings. However, these accounts often come with restrictions around withdrawals before the age of 59.5 years and early withdrawals can incur penalties. Nevertheless, the Roth IRA offers a unique loophole that can be advantageous for early retirees.

Unlike traditional IRAs and 401(k) accounts, which provide a tax deduction on contributions but tax withdrawals, Roth IRAs follow the opposite approach. Contributions to a Roth IRA are made with after-tax dollars, meaning you pay taxes upfront. However, qualified withdrawals from the account, including both contributions and earnings, are tax-free. The distinct feature of Roth IRAs that benefits early retirees is the ability to withdraw contributions (but not earnings) at any time without penalties or taxes. This is because you've already paid taxes on the money you contributed. This flexibility can provide a valuable tax-free income source during early retirement years before reaching the typical age of retirement.

Roth conversion ladder

The Roth conversion ladder is a strategy often employed by those who aim to retire early, enabling them to access their retirement funds before the traditional retirement age without incurring penalties. This strategy is a multistep process that requires careful planning and understanding of the associated tax implications. The basic premise involves converting money from a traditional IRA to a Roth IRA.

To set up a Roth conversion ladder, you start by converting a portion of your traditional IRA to a Roth IRA. This converted amount is considered income and is therefore taxable in the year of conversion. The purpose of the ladder is to spread these conversions (and the associated tax liability) over several years, keeping your income in a lower tax bracket. The critical aspect of this strategy is the Roth IRA's unique rule regarding the withdrawal of conversions. When the funds have been in the Roth IRA for a period of five years, they can be withdrawn penalty-free and tax-free, regardless of your age. This is different from the withdrawal rules for earnings in a Roth IRA, which typically require the account holder to be 59.5 years old and the account to be open for at least five years to avoid taxes and penalties.

Therefore, to use this strategy effectively, early retirees need to plan ahead. For example, if you plan to retire in five years, you would start the Roth conversions now so that in five years, you have access to those funds. Each year, you would convert another portion of your traditional IRA, creating a "ladder" of conversions that become available for penalty-free withdrawal each subsequent year. This provides a steady stream of income during the early years of retirement.

Strategic withdrawals and the 72(t) rule

The 72(t) rule is a lesser-known provision within the U.S. Internal Revenue Code that can be a strategic tool for early retirees. This rule provides a method for individuals to access funds within their retirement accounts before reaching the age of 59.5 without incurring the standard 10% early withdrawal penalty. The 72(t) rule allows for substantially equal periodic payments (SEPPs) to be withdrawn from your retirement accounts.

The amount of these payments is determined based on your life expectancy and the balance within your retirement account. The IRS offers three methods to calculate SEPPs, the required minimum distribution method, the fixed amortization method and the fixed annuitization method. These methods are specifically designed to ensure that the entire retirement account isn't depleted prematurely.

However, initiating SEPPs under the 72(t) rule is not a decision to be taken lightly. Once you commence these withdrawals, you are obligated to continue them for a minimum of five years or until you reach the age of 59.5, whichever comes later. For instance, if you start the SEPPs at age 57, you'll have to continue until you are 62. If the payments are altered or stopped prematurely, you'll have to pay the 10% early withdrawal penalty retroactively on all withdrawals made prior to age 59.5, along with any interest due.

Affordable Care Act subsidies

The Affordable Care Act (ACA), also known as Obamacare, provides subsidies to help lower-income individuals and families afford health insurance. These subsidies are based on a sliding scale, with the aim of ensuring that people with less income pay a smaller percentage of their income on health insurance premiums. For early retirees who are not yet eligible for Medicare and who need to obtain health insurance through the marketplace, these subsidies can be a significant factor in managing health care costs. Income for the purposes of the ACA includes not just earnings from work, but also withdrawals from retirement accounts, capital gains and other sources.

The subsidies are calculated based on modified adjusted gross income (MAGI), which is your household's adjusted gross income plus any tax-exempt Social Security, interest and foreign income. It's important to be aware that ACA uses a specific definition of MAGI, which may differ from other uses of MAGI in the tax code. To qualify for premium tax credits, your MAGI must be between

100% and 400% of the federal poverty level (FPL) for your household size. If you fall within these thresholds, you could receive substantial premium tax credits to help lower your insurance costs. The exact amount of the subsidies will depend on where your income falls within the applicable range, with lower income levels receiving larger subsidies.

However, exceeding the 400% FPL limit by even a small amount could result in losing all subsidies, leading to a significant increase in premium costs. This is often referred to as the "ACA cliff." Therefore, carefully managing your income to stay within the qualifying range can save you a significant amount of money on health insurance premiums. Strategies for managing income to optimize ACA subsidies could include controlling the timing and amount of withdrawals from retirement accounts, offsetting capital gains with capital losses and making contributions to HSAs or other accounts that reduce your MAGI. It's also important to remember that these income thresholds are updated annually, so you will need to review your income strategy each year.

Health Care

Health care is a significant consideration for anyone planning to retire early, especially in the United States. Since most U.S. citizens don't qualify for Medicare until they turn 65, early retirees need to find other ways to cover their health care costs. This section will guide you through the various options available.

The Affordable Care Act (ACA), also know as Obamacare, created health insurance marketplaces in which individuals can buy health insurance. Plans offered on these market-places are categorized into four "metal" tiers—bronze, silver, gold and platinum—each with different premiums, deductibles and out-of-pocket maximums. Subsidies are available for those with incomes between 100% and 400% of the FPL, which can significantly lower the cost of insurance.

If you retire early, you may have the option to continue your employer-provided health insurance for a limited period through COBRA (Consolidated Omnibus Budget Reconciliation Act). While COBRA allows you to keep the same coverage, you'll have to pay the full premium cost plus a small administrative fee. This option can be expensive, but it might be worth considering if you prefer to keep your current coverage or have ongoing medical issues.

Health sharing plans are cooperative groups in which members share each other's health care costs. While these plans can be less expensive than traditional health insurance, they are not insurance and do not have to meet ACA requirements. It's important to read the fine print and understand what is and isn't covered before choosing this option.

Short-term health insurance plans offer coverage for a limited period, typically one year with the option to renew for two additional years. While these plans can be less expensive than traditional health insurance, they do not have to cover preexisting conditions or the essential health benefits required by the ACA, such as preventive care and mental health services.

Direct primary care (DPC) is a model in which patients pay their doctor or clinic directly in the form of a periodic fee, providing patients with access to comprehensive primary care services. DPC can be an affordable way to cover routine medical care, but it's not insurance and doesn't cover hospitalizations, specialist visits or other high-cost care. DPC is often used in combination with a high-deductible health plan or health sharing plan.

After 65, U.S. citizens or permanent residents become eligible for Medicare, the federal health insurance program. Medicare is divided into parts A through D. Medicare Part A covers hospital stays, skilled nursing facility stays and some home health care. Most people don't pay a monthly premium for Part A if they or their spouse paid Medicare taxes while working. Medicare Part B covers certain doctors' services, outpatient care, medical supplies and preventive services. A monthly premium is required for Part B. An alternative to Original Medicare (Parts A and B), Medicare Part C (Medicare Advantage Plans) are offered by private companies approved by Medicare and cover all services covered under Parts A and B and usually also offer prescription drug coverage. Medicare Part D covers prescription drug costs, offered through private insurance companies that follow rules set by Medicare.

Medigap policies, also known as Medicare Supplement Insurance policies, are sold by private companies and can help cover some of the health care costs that original Medicare doesn't cover, like copayments, coinsurance and deductibles. It's important to note that Medigap policies don't work with Medicare Advantage Plans, only with original Medicare.

Medicare provides limited coverage for long-term care services, such as nursing homes or assisted living facilities. Therefore, some retirees opt for long-term care insurance, which covers services generally not covered by health insurance, Medicare or Medicaid. These policies can be costly but can provide peace of mind for those concerned about affording long-term care.

HSAs are a particularly powerful tool for managing health care expenses, especially in retirement. Let's review some of the key aspects we have already discussed in Chapter 4 (page 62) and how they particularly apply to retirees.

HSAs are uniquely designed for individuals with high-deductible health plans. They provide an opportunity to make tax-deductible contributions, allow the money to grow tax-free and permit tax-free withdrawals for qualified medical expenses. This triple tax advantage makes HSAs a beneficial tool for long-term health care savings.

While you can't contribute to an HSA once you enroll in Medicare at age 65, you can use the funds in your HSA to pay for Medicare premiums, co-pays and a portion of long-term care insurance premiums, all tax-free. There is no required minimum distribution for HSAs as there is for certain retirement accounts. This means you can let the money grow as long as you want, providing a tax-advantaged health care fund well into retirement. HSAs can serve as a supplemental retirement account with a focus on health care costs, a significant consideration for any retiree but particularly relevant for those who retire early and may need a bridge for health care coverage before Medicare eligibility.

Remember to plan for out-of-pocket maximums and unexpected health costs, like surgeries or hospital stays, which could significantly impact your budget. A well-crafted retirement plan should include a contingency for unexpected health care expenses to ensure financial security in retirement. Health care considerations in retirement are complex and vary significantly based on individual circumstances. A thorough understanding of your options, costs and potential risks will help you develop a more robust and resilient retirement plan.

Social Security

In the United States, the Social Security program is a federal initiative offering financial benefits to retired persons, those with disabilities and their beneficiaries. Dating back to 1935 and the Social Security Act, this program has offered a financial lifeline to countless Americans. Its funding relies on payroll taxes, the Federal Insurance Contributions Act (FICA) tax, which both employers and employees pay into, with self-employed folks carrying the full weight. The funds gathered are then distributed to those currently benefiting from the program.

The main component of Social Security is the retirement benefit. Eligible to those who've paid into the system for at least a decade and have hit the age of 62, it acts as an income supplement. Full benefits kick in between the ages of 65 and 67, depending on your birth year, and the amount you receive hinges on your past earnings and the age you decide to claim your benefits. If you can hold off on claiming your benefits until you reach 70, you'll enjoy an even heftier monthly payout, thanks to the "delayed retirement credits" that boost your benefit amount for each year you wait.

However, Social Security wasn't built to be a retiree's sole source of income. It was designed to complement personal savings, pensions and investments. Therefore, while it can certainly form part of your retirement income plan, it shouldn't be the sole pillar.

Here's the catch: according to the Social Security Administration's predictions, if the system doesn't see changes soon, the combined reserves of the Old-Age, Survivors, and Disability Insurance (OASDI) programs are expected to run dry by 2035. Once this happens, the system will only be able to cover about 79% of promised benefits, using ongoing payroll tax revenue. Therefore, unless policy changes or tax increases intervene, there could be cuts to benefits.

In light of this, it would be wise to start claiming Social Security benefits at the earliest opportunity, age 62. While claiming early leads to smaller monthly payments, it does mean you'll be receiving these payments for longer. The idea is that, given the system's uncertain future, it's better to start claiming whatever benefits you can as soon as you're able. The "break-even" point, when waiting for larger benefits outweighs the total amount you'd get by starting earlier, usually doesn't come until your late 70s or early 80s, an age not everyone reaches.

Ultimately, while Social Security can still feature in retirement planning, these potential changes highlight the importance of personal savings and investments when planning for a financially secure future. Proactively building a diverse and solid retirement portfolio can give you more control over your financial future, regardless of the fate of the Social Security system.

Estate Planning

Navigating the aftermath of a family member's death when there wasn't a proper estate plan in place was an absolute nightmare. My family was in shock, mourning the sudden loss of our loved one, and it was during this painful period that we also had to face the daunting reality of navigating legal and financial matters without any clear direction from a will or estate plan. Without a will, our loved one's estate was thrust into the probate process. It was a bewildering maze that took more than two years to resolve. The endless paperwork, court appearances and red tape created a significant strain on our family during an already challenging time.

The probate process was not only time-consuming but also expensive. Legal fees and court costs quickly added up, draining resources that could have been part of the inheritance. Beyond the financial burden, the most significant impact was the emotional toll. The stress of dealing with the probate process and the sheer amount of time it all took only compounded our grief. Having a comprehensive estate plan could have spared my family much of this pain. It would have expedited the legal process, clearly outlined the division of assets, reduced the financial strain and, most importantly, allowed us to focus on supporting each other during a time of loss. It's not just about the assets; it's about easing the burden for your loved ones during a difficult time.

Both wills and trusts are legal tools used for estate planning and the management and distribution of your assets. However, they serve different functions and come with their own set of pros and cons. Understanding these differences will help you make an informed decision about what's best for your unique circumstances.

At its core, a will is a legal instrument that allows you to dictate how your assets will be distributed upon your demise. It provides a roadmap for how you want your personal and financial affairs to be handled. A will can encompass everything from real estate and financial assets to personal belongings like jewelry, cars and family heirlooms. Beyond your possessions, if you have minor children, in your will is the document you can designate guardians for them. Additionally, a will allows you to name an executor, someone who will be responsible for carrying out your instructions, managing your estate and guiding it through probate if necessary. Creating a will is generally less complicated and less expensive than creating a trust and you can change or revoke your will at any time before your death. However, wills must go through probate, a court-supervised process of distributing your estate. This process can be time-consuming, costly and is a matter of public record.

While a will serves to manage your affairs after death, a living will (also known as an advance health care directive) serves an equal role during your life. A living will comes into play when you are alive but unable to communicate your medical preferences due to a severe illness or incapacitation. A living will contains directives about your medical treatment and interventions you would like to receive or avoid. This could include your wishes regarding life-prolonging measures, resuscitation orders, artificial nutrition and hydration, as well as pain management. The primary purpose of a living will is to ensure that your health care preferences are respected, even when you can't communicate them yourself. It can bring peace of mind, knowing that you have a say in your medical care and can prevent potential disagreements among family members about your treatment. Often, as part of your living will, you can designate a health care proxy or health care power of attorney, someone you trust to make medical decisions on your behalf if you're unable to do so.

A trust, on the other hand, provides much more versatile legal arrangements that can play a crucial role in your estate planning strategy. Through a trust, you (as the grantor) give another party (the trustee) the authority to hold and manage assets for the benefit of one or more beneficiaries. Trusts offer several benefits, including potential tax advantages, probate avoidance and the ability to specify the terms of distribution, such as releasing funds when a child reaches a certain age. The downside is that trusts are generally more complex and costly to set up than wills. They require ongoing management. Some types of trusts, once created, cannot be changed or revoked.

Choosing between a will and a trust, or using both, depends on your personal circumstances, your assets and your estate planning goals. For instance, if you have a relatively small estate and your main concern is naming guardians for your children, a will might suffice. If you want to avoid probate or have more complex distribution plans, a trust might be the better option. You should consult with an estate planning attorney to understand which option is best suited for your needs.

Understanding the potential tax implications of your estate is another essential part of comprehensive estate planning. Depending on the size and nature of your assets, your estate may be subject to various taxes, including federal estate taxes and possibly state inheritance or estate taxes. By properly planning, you can optimize your estate to minimize the impact of these taxes, ensuring that more of your assets go to your chosen beneficiaries. In 2023, estates with a gross asset value exceeding $12.92 million (or $25.84 million for married couples) were subject to federal estate tax.

These exemption thresholds are adjusted annually for inflation, so be sure to check the current levels. The tax rate for estates above the exemption amount can reach up to 40%.

One common strategy for reducing your taxable estate is gifting. The federal government allows an annual gift tax exclusion, which was $17,000 per recipient for 2023. This means you can give up to $17,000 to as many individuals as you want each year without impacting your estate tax exemption amount. In addition to federal taxes, your estate might also be subject to state taxes. Twelve states and the District of Columbia impose an estate tax and six states have an inheritance tax. Maryland has both. These taxes can apply to much smaller estates than the federal estate tax, with some starting at levels as low as $1 million.

Chapter 9

REFLECTIONS

The true beauty of financial independence and retiring early rests not solely in monetary security but the profound freedom it offers. With this privilege comes the ability to explore paths previously unattainable or impractical due to monetary constraints. With financial independence, a world of options opens up to you, where the scope of possibility is only defined by your passion and interest, not your wallet.

Maybe the road to fulfillment for you lies in your current occupation, and financial independence simply provides an added layer of security and choice, allowing you to continue working on your own terms. Alternatively, you might seize this chance to immerse yourself in a long-cherished hobby or passion project, devoting your time and energy to something that truly kindles your spirit. The door might also lead to a lower-paying job that, while not financially rewarding, provides a sense of gratification and joy far beyond monetary compensation. Your journey might even veer toward more altruistic paths such as joining organizations like the Peace Corps, initiating a non-profit venture or dedicating substantial time to volunteer work. Your aspirations, whether they are to explore; create; serve; or simply unwind, relax and revel in the tranquility of having nothing to do at all, are all possible.

The gift of financial autonomy comes with the unique privilege of prioritizing one's health, a precious asset that is often on the back burner amidst the whirlwind of work commitments. It's a well-known saying, yet so profoundly true: "Health is wealth." Working in high-pressure environments can often take a heavy toll on both physical and mental well-being, leaving little time or energy for self-care. But the scales tip favorably once the chains of work-related stress are broken. You can finally focus on restoring and revitalizing your health, offering you a chance to prioritize your well-being, which had perhaps been lingering at the edges of your busy work life. No more excuses to delay that gym membership or sideline a balanced, nutritious diet. No more sleepless nights of work at the expense of restful sleep.

I can state without a shadow of doubt that the financial autonomy I now enjoy has enriched my life in ways that are far more profound than the mere absence of a nine-to-five commitment. Foremost among these enriching experiences is the sheer abundance of quality time I now get to share with my loved ones. Freed from the shackles of a rigid work schedule, I'm able to immerse myself in the simple, delightful rhythm of daily life with my wife and our two spirited sons. We've replaced hurried breakfasts with leisurely morning meals, punctuated with laughter and stories. Weekdays no longer usher in a rush to beat traffic but beckon us outdoors to enjoy the splendor of our local parks. These outings, filled with laughter, exploration and genuine connection, have become a cherished ritual for us.

We've plunged into a wide array of activities, each a little universe of learning and discovery on its own. Whether we're perfecting our swings on the golf course, ducking and weaving in boxing gloves, chasing tennis balls or crabbing in bibs and rubber boots by the sea, our shared experiences have created a vivid collection of memories. One of the most understated yet significant perks of F.I.R.E. is the sheer convenience it offers. Simple tasks like grocery shopping or running errands have transformed from tiresome chores that needed to be squeezed into my schedule, into enjoyable, relaxed excursions. With the ability to avoid peak hours, traffic has become an outdated concept for us, making even the most mundane tasks surprisingly pleasant.

When I was a full-time worker, the reality of parenthood struck me with its demanding nature. The relentless task of raising young children was a constant tug-of-war between my professional commitments and my role as a parent. But here's the thing: parenting, with all its challenges, was a commitment I wouldn't trade for anything. The labor of love it required was fulfilling in a way that no corporate achievement could ever match. And now I'm able to fully embrace the joy and privilege of being present in my children's lives. No longer am I bound to parcel out my energy in accordance with a corporate schedule, trying to reserve scraps of enthusiasm and attention for my kids after a draining day at work. I'm free to devote my most productive hours to guiding and nurturing them, relishing the opportunity to witness their formative years.

However, F.I.R.E. is not solely about indulging in freedom; it's a mindful balance between personal satisfaction and continued growth. It's a pivot from pursuing corporate success to setting personal aspirations, fostering new achievements and consistently striving for a well-rounded life. Our lives require a balanced approach. After all, the pursuit of happiness in a life of financial independence is as much about the journey as it is about the destination. It's about the consistent striving for a fulfilling and well-rounded life, not just the initial thrill of breaking away from the corporate grind. This mindset led me to explore an unexpected and playful challenge from my wife, turning a lighthearted competition into a viral success story and eventually culminating in writing this book.

Whether it's seizing the chance to explore a cherished hobby, deepening our relationships with loved ones or embracing an unexpected path like a viral social media adventure, the autonomy achieved through financial independence enables us to live authentically. As you embark on this path, remember that your pursuit is not merely about freedom from financial burdens but a continual exploration of self, a balance between pleasure and purpose and an opportunity to craft a life that resonates with your truest self.

The story of financial independence is not just about an end goal but a transformative journey that starts with a single step toward a more fulfilled life. May this book serve as your guide, and may your journey be as enriching and vibrant as the life you seek.

We all have friends, family members and acquaintances who might be navigating their financial paths with a degree of uncertainty. I encourage you to share this book with others who might find it valuable, empowering them to take control of their financial future.

Last, I express my deepest gratitude for embarking on this journey with me. Your thirst for knowledge is an inspiration. Visit www.frankniu.com/extras for additional resources, tools and guidance. Your commitment to improvement is not the end but the beginning of a new chapter in your life.

ACKNOWLEDGMENTS

First, I'd like to acknowledge my two wonderful sons. You are the fuel to my fire, the laughter in my life and the inspiration for so much of what I do. Your inquisitive minds and youthful spirits make every day an adventure. I hope you read this book one day and understand the values I've tried to instill within its pages.

To my parents, who have been the pillars of my life, thank you. Your unfailing support, love and guidance set me on this path. I owe you a debt of gratitude for teaching me about the importance of diligence, the power of education and the value of humility.

My beautiful wife, Annie, you are the heart of everything I do. You have stood by me, believed in me and been my confidante and cheerleader in this long, arduous process. This journey would have been less bright and far less enjoyable without you by my side.

A massive thank you to my publisher, Page Street Publishing Co., for believing in this book and helping me bring it to life. Your faith in my vision and your hard work have made this dream a reality.

To my remarkable editor, Marissa Giambelluca, your sharp eye and insightful suggestions have been invaluable. Your guidance has not only enhanced this book, but also has contributed significantly to my growth as a writer.

A special thanks to Emma Hardy, whose creativity and talent shaped the cover and book design. Her penchant for detail and artistic flair have added an aesthetic dimension that truly complements the content within.

To my friends, your support has been unwavering. You've been my sounding board, my critics and my personal cheer squad. You've lent me your ears, given me your time and enriched this book with your expertise. This journey has been all the more meaningful because I had you to share it with.

Finally, to my readers, thank you. This book was written for you and your journey toward financial independence. Your curiosity, engagement and passion for learning are what make all the late nights and early mornings worth it. I am humbled by your trust and hope you find this book a useful tool in your journey toward financial independence.

ABOUT THE AUTHOR

Frank Niu retired at the age of 30 after a successful career as a software engineer in the technology industry. Afterward, he swiftly transformed his passion for technology, finance and career planning into a thriving social media presence.

With more than a million followers across various platforms, Frank's insights have resonated with audiences worldwide. His expertise and unique perspective have earned him features in notable publications like *Business Insider*, *The Wall Street Journal*, *Yahoo*, *Fox* and *Entrepreneur*.

But Frank's life isn't all about tech and finance. A dedicated family man, he's the proud father of two and is happily married to Annie Niu. In his free time, he immerses himself in hobbies that include playing video games, watching anime and reading fantasy novels.

Connect with Frank on social media to keep up with his latest thoughts, adventures and advice. Find him on Instagram and Twitter at @niu_xiaofei, and on TikTok and YouTube at @frankniu.

Whether you're interested in insights on early retirement, professional growth or exploring engaging hobbies that complement a fulfilling life, Frank's diverse interests and deep knowledge make him a figure to watch in the worlds of technology, finance and beyond. Find out more at www.frankniu.com.

INDEX